Cycle
Tours

Chilterns, Hertfordshire & Essex

Nick Cotton

Publisher: Cycle Tours is a joint venture between
CycleCity Guides and Cordee

CycleCity Guides
The Welsh Mill
Parkhill Drive
Frome
BA11 2LE
T: +44 (0)1373 453533

info@cyclecityguides.co.uk
www.cyclecityguides.co.uk

Cordee
11 Jacknell Road
Dodwells Bridge Industrial Estate
Hinckley
LE10 3BS
T: +44 (0)1455 611 185

charlie@cordee.co.uk
www.cordee.co.uk

ISBN: 978-1904207580

Printed by: Victoria Litho
Picture credits: Nick Cotton

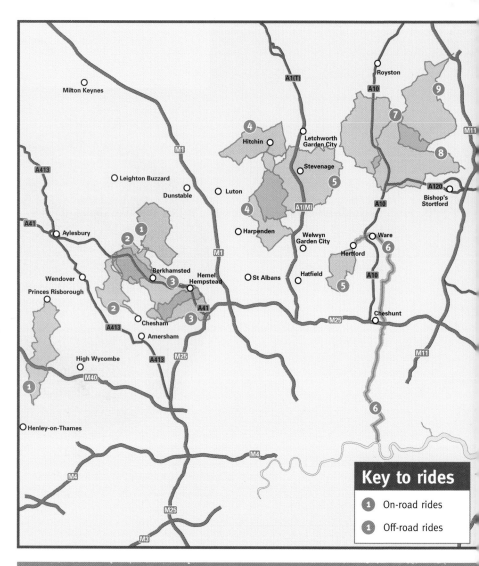

Key to rides

1	On-road rides
1	Off-road rides

Off-road rides

	Ride number & title	Page	Distance	Grade
1	Aldbury & the Icknield Way	98	20m (32km)	▲▲▲▲▲
2	Woodland above Tring & Berkhamsted	104	17m (27km)	▲▲▲▲
3	Hemel Hempstead & Grand Union Canal	110	21m (34km)	▲▲▲
4	Great Offley & the Icknield Way	116	20m (32km)	▲▲▲
5	Southwest from Hertford	122	15m (24km)	▲

Quick reference chart

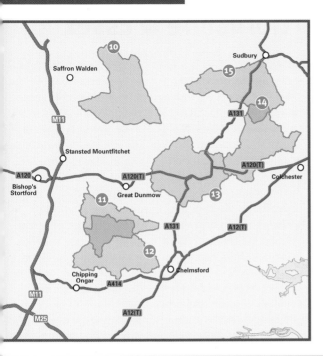

Grades

▲
Easy

▲▲
Easy / Moderate

▲▲▲
Moderate

▲▲▲▲
Moderate / Strenuous

▲▲▲▲▲
Strenuous

The grade is based on the amount of climbing involved and, for off-road routes, the roughness of the surface rather than the distance covered.

On-road rides

Chilterns, Hertfordshire & Essex

The area to the north and west of London, including all or part of Buckinghamshire, Hertfordshire and Essex, provides some excellent and varied cycling: from the challenges of the steep wooded escarpment of the Chilterns in the west to the gentle gradients on the network of quiet lanes in Hertfordshire and north Essex.

The Chilterns rise to over 800ft (245m) at several points along the escarpment as it runs northeast from the River Thames at Goring towards Dunstable and Luton. Three of the five off-road rides use the fine network of tracks that explore the area's famous beech woodlands, often forming a great green tree cathedral, especially stunning in late spring when the woodland floor is carpeted with bluebells and in late autumn as the colours change. These rides, and also the other two mountain bike rides near to Hitchin and Hertford, are best done after a few dry days from late spring to late autumn. They can be very hard going in mid-winter.

Three of the road rides also explore the Chiltern woodlands, one from Princes Risborough and two around Tring. For those of you looking for easy rides in this area, try the section of the Grand Union Canal between Tring and Hemel Hempstead, most of which has been brought up to a standard easily passable on road bikes. Another canal which is explored from end to end is the Lee Navigation between Hertford and Limehouse Basin in London: the towpath is one of the best in the whole country with lots of pubs and cafés to explore along its length, offering a flat and traffic-free ride up to 28 miles one way.

East of the Chilterns the rides explore the network of quiet lanes that criss-cross this gently rolling, predominantly arable landscape. Small villages of thatched and half-timbered houses seem to vie with each other for the splendour of their village signs, often intricately carved and painted. Another distinctive feature of the area is the pargeting or plasterwork on the façades of the buildings. You will normally find a pub in the larger villages so take your time and enjoy the day.

So ... plenty of rides to try out whether you live in the area, are visiting friends or family or you fancy a break from London. Use the shortcuts if you are pushed for time or put two or more rides together for a big day out.

Other useful information

Easy, traffic-free cycling for families and novices
If you want a ride that is also suitable for children or 'novice' cyclists try some of these easier traffic-free routes on dismantled railways, canal towpaths or in Forestry Commission holdings.

Canals
1. Grand Union Canal
The best stretches of towpath lie between Denham Country Park (north of Uxbridge) and Tring. A long section of the Grand Union Canal is followed in Ride 3 (page 20) from Tring to Hemel Hempstead.

2. Lee Navigation
The whole length of the towpath, from Hertford to Limehouse Basin at its junction with the River Thames, is described in Ride 6 (page 38).

Railway paths
1. Nickey Line
3 miles from Harpenden to Hemel Hempstead.
See: **www.stalbans.gov.uk** and search **'Nickey Line'**.

2. Ebury Way
3 miles from Rickmansworth to Watford
See: **www.watford.gov.uk** and search **'Ebury Way cycle leaflet'**.

3. Ayot Greenway
4 miles from Wheathampstead to Ayot St Peter.
See: **www.hertsdirect.org** and search **'Ayot Green Way'**.

4. Albanway
7 miles from Hatfield to St Albans
See: **www.hertsdirect.org** and search **'Alban Way'**.

5. Cole Green Way
4 miles from Hertford to Cole Green
See: **www.hertsdirect.org** and search **'Cole Green Way'**.

6. Flitch Way
3 miles from Braintree towards Great Dunmow
See: **www.essex.gov.uk** and search **'Flitch Way leaflet'**.

7. Wivenhoe Trail
5 miles from Colchester to Wivenhoe.
See: **www.cyclecolchester.org.uk**

Woodland
1. Epping Forest
Many trails criss-cross the woodland.
See **www.cityoflondon.gov.uk** and search **'Epping Forest Cycling Map'**.

2. Wendover Woods
The woodland is very beautiful but the hills are steep! See: **www.forestry.gov.uk/WendoverWoods**

Sustrans and the National Cycle Network
Go to **www.sustrans.org.uk** click on **'Sustrans near you'** then **'East of England'** for Hertfordshire and Essex and **'South East'** for the Chilterns and Buckinghamshire. There are downloads, details of free leaflets and details of NCN routes in the region.

Cycle shops in the area
See
www.ibuckinghamshire.co.uk/local/cycle-shops/
www.ihertfordshire.co.uk/local/cycle-shops/
www.iessex.co.uk/local/cycle-shops/
www.thecyclepeople.com

3

Legend to 1:50,000 maps

Roads & paths

Motorway

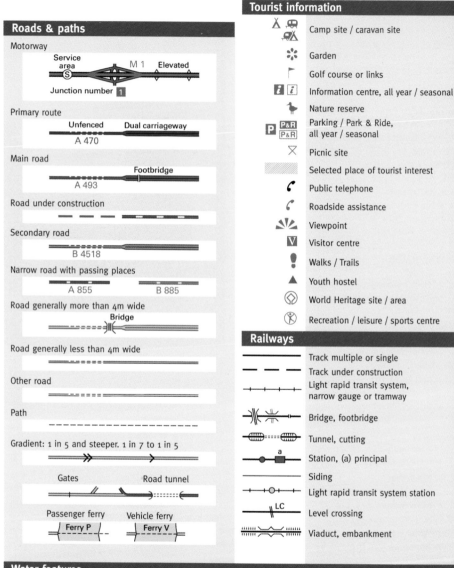

Primary route

Main road

Road under construction

Secondary road

Narrow road with passing places

Road generally more than 4m wide

Road generally less than 4m wide

Other road

Path

Gradient: 1 in 5 and steeper. 1 in 7 to 1 in 5

Gates   Road tunnel

Passenger ferry   Vehicle ferry

Tourist information

- Camp site / caravan site
- Garden
- Golf course or links
- Information centre, all year / seasonal
- Nature reserve
- Parking / Park & Ride, all year / seasonal
- Picnic site
- Selected place of tourist interest
- Public telephone
- Roadside assistance
- Viewpoint
- Visitor centre
- Walks / Trails
- Youth hostel
- World Heritage site / area
- Recreation / leisure / sports centre

Railways

- Track multiple or single
- Track under construction
- Light rapid transit system, narrow gauge or tramway
- Bridge, footbridge
- Tunnel, cutting
- Station, (a) principal
- Siding
- Light rapid transit system station
- Level crossing
- Viaduct, embankment

Water features

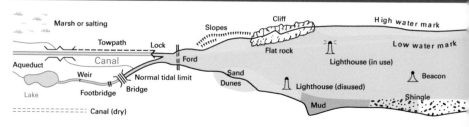

4

General features

⁝⁝⁝⁝⁝ ⁝⁝⁝⁝⁝	Cutting, embankment
	Landfill site
	Coniferous wood
	Non-coniferous wood
	Mixed wood
	Orchard
	Park or ornamental ground
	Forestry Commission land
	National Trust - always open
	National Trust - limited access, observe local signs
	National Trust for Scotland - always open
	National Trust for Scotland - limited access, observe local signs
ʌ — ʌ — ʌ	Electricity transmission line (pylons shown at standard spacing)
> - -> - ->	Pipe line (arrow indicates direction of flow)
	Building
	Important building (selected)
	Bus or coach station
	Glass structure
Ⓗ	Hospital
	Place of worship with tower
	Place of worship with spire, dome or minaret
+	Place of worship
	Mast
	Wind pump / wind turbine
	Windmill with or without sails
	Graticule intersection at 5' intervals

Rock features

Outcrop
Cliff
Scree

Public rights of way
(not applicable in Scotland)

·················	Footpath
—·—·—·—·—	Restricted byway
— — — — —	Bridleway
-+-+-+-+-+-	Byway open to all traffic

Public rights of way shown have been taken from local authority definitive maps and later amendments. The symbols show the defined route so far as the scale of mapping will allow.

The representation on this map of any other road, track or path is no evidence of the existence of a right of way.

Other public access

· · · ·	Other route with public access
◆ ◆ ◆	National Trail, European Long Distance Path, Long Distance Route, selected Recreational Routes
● ● ●	On-road cycle route
○ ○ ○	Off-road cycle route
4	National Cycle Network Number
8	Regional Cycle Network Number
Danger Area	Firing and test ranges in the area Danger! Observe warning notices

Boundaries

+ — + — +	National
+ ·· + ·· + ·· +	District
— · — · — · —	County, region or island area
	National Park

Abbreviations

CH	Clubhouse
PH	Public house
PC	Public convenience (in rural area)
TH	Town Hall, Guildhall or equivalent
CG	Cattle grid
P	Post office
MP	Milepost
MS	Mile stone

Antiquities

+	Position of antiquity that cannot be drawn to scale
☆ ····	Visible earthwork
VILLA	Roman
Castle	Non-Roman
⚔	Battlefield (with date)

Heights

═══50═══	Contours are at 10 metre vertical intervals
·144	Heights are to the nearest metre above mean sea level

Heights shown close to a triangulation pillar refer to the station height at ground level and not necessarily to the summit

5

Abbreviations and instructions

Instructions are given concisely to make them easy to follow while out riding. Remember to read one or two instructions ahead so that you do not miss a turning. This is most likely when you have to turn off a road / track you have been following for a while and are marked **Easy to miss** to warn you.

If there appears to be a contradiction between the instructions and what you actually see, alway refer to the map. There are many reasons why, over the course of time, instructions may be subject to change with new roads, new junctions and new signposts.

Directions (all directions are given in bold)

L	left
R	right
SA	straight ahead
bear **L** or **R**	a turn which is less than 90 degrees (right-angle) at a fork in the road or on a sharp bend so that your course appears to be straight ahead; this is often written as 'in effect **SA**'
sharp **L** or **R**	a turn more acute than a right-angle
L or **R** sharply back on yourself	almost a U-turn
R then **L**	normally a T-junction where the next turn is visible from the first
R then first **L**	the second turning may be some distance from the first, ie '**R** then after ½ mile first **L**'

Junctions

T-j	T-junction, a junction where you have to give way
X-roads	crossroads, a junction where you may or may not have to give way
offset X-roads	the four roads are not in the form of a perfect cross and you will have to turn left then right, or vice versa, to continue the route

Signs

'Placename 2'	the words in quotation marks are those that appear on the signs, the numbers indicate the distance in miles unless stated otherwise
(NS)	not signposted

Instructions

An example of an easy instruction is:

4 At T-j at end of Smith Road by the White Swan Inn turn **R** on Brown Street 'Greentown 2, Redville 3'

There is more information in this instruction than you would normally need but things do change: pubs may close down and signs may be replaced, removed or vandalised.

An example of a difficult instruction is:

8 **Easy to miss:** shortly after the brow of the hill, on fast descent, first **R** (NS)

As you can see, there is no T-junction or 'Give Way' sign to halt you in your tracks, no signpost indicating where the right turn will take you and in addition you are picking up speed on a downhill, so you need to have your wits about you not to miss the turning.

Overview pages

Start
This is the suggested start point, coinciding with instruction 1 on the map. There is no reason why you should not start at another point if it is more convenient.

Busy roads
These rides aim to keep to an absolute minimum time spent on busy roads but there are sometimes unavoidable sections where lane networks do not neatly link together. These busy roads are mentioned so that you are mentally prepared to deal with traffic, especially if there are children or less experienced cyclists in the group.

Off-road sections (on-road rides)
Occasionally a short distance on a traffic-free cyclepath, bridleway, byway or unclassified road can offer an alternative to a busy road. As the surfaces are not sealed you may encounter puddles or muddy water, especially in winter or after prolonged rain.

Terrain
This brief description of the terrain covered by the route should be read in conjunction with the cross-profile diagram at the foot of the page to help you plan your journey.

Distance
The distance (shown in miles and kilometres) is, of course, that from the beginning to the end of the ride. However, if you wish to shorten the ride because of tiredness, mechanical problems, a change in the weather or simply lack of time then the maps enable you to do so.

Grade
There are five grades of difficulty:
Easy
Easy / Moderate
Moderate
Moderate / Strenuous
Strenuous
The grade is based on the amount of climbing involved and, for off-road routes, the roughness of the surface rather than the distance covered.

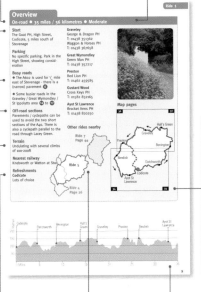

Map pages
Route overviews show how the maps have been laid out on the pages. Page numbers are shown in the corners. The diagrams show start points, route direction and some of the villages on or near the route.

Other rides nearby
Schematic map showing where nearby rides overlap. Shorter or longer rides can be created by mixing and matching rides.

Cross-profile
Shows heights in metres and distance travelled. Places along the route are shown.

Refreshments
More than three pubs or a mixture of pubs, cafés and tearooms in any one place is indicated by 'Lots of choice'. Otherwise, names of pubs, cafés and tearooms are listed, where possible with telephone numbers so that you can call ahead to check on opening times and when food is served.

South from Princes Risborough through the Chilterns to Hambleden

The Chilterns provide some of the very best cycling close to London. Turning down yet another tiny lane in the midst of beechwoods it is hard to imagine that the centre of London is only 30 miles away. There are many pretty villages built of brick and flint and a concentration of excellent pubs, even in the most unlikely of places. This ride forms a cigar-shaped loop and runs roughly north-south from Princes Risborough up over Bledlow Ridge. It continues through glorious woodland down the Hambleden valley, passing the villages of Finges and Skirmett to Hambleden itself. The cakes at the café / village store in Hambleden are highly recommended! The village has frequently been used as a film set. It is also famous as the home village of William Henry Smith, founder of WH Smith and the birthplace of Lord Cardigan, leader of the ill-judged Charge of the Light Brigade. A climb out of the Hambleden valley, including one short but very steep section, brings you up to the ridge. It is worth diverting to West Wycombe village with its collection of architectural styles and its church set in the middle of an Iron Age fort. West Wycombe was also the location of Sir Francis Dashwood's infamous Hellfire Club in the mid-18th century. A last climb takes you past the windmill at Lacey Green, where the views from the escarpment are spectacular. A fast woodland descent takes you back to Princes Risborough.

Overview
On-road ● 29 miles / 47 kilometres ● Moderate / Strenuous

Start
High Street, Princes Risborough

Parking
Follow signs from the clock tower onto Church Street

Busy roads
Pavements / cyclepaths can be used to avoid the two short sections of the A40. There is also a cyclepath parallel to the road through Lacey Green

Terrain
Hilly with two noticeable climbs from Princes Risborough up over Bledlow Ridge to the A40 then several more climbs on the way back from Hambleden reaching the ride's highpoint above Princes Risborough

Nearest railway
Princes Risborough

Refreshments
Princes Risborough
Lots of choice

Radnage
Crown PH
T: 01494 482301

Fingest
Chequers Inn
T: 01491 638335

Skirmett
Frog PH
T: 01491 638996

Hambleden
Stag & Huntsman
T: 01481 571227
Café (tables outside)
at village stores

Lacey Green
Pink & Lily PH
T: 01494 488308

Loosley Row
Whip Inn
T: 01844 344060

Map pages

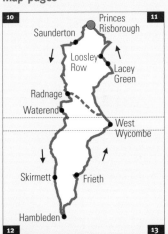

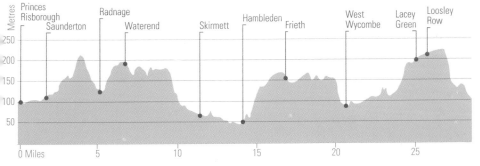

9

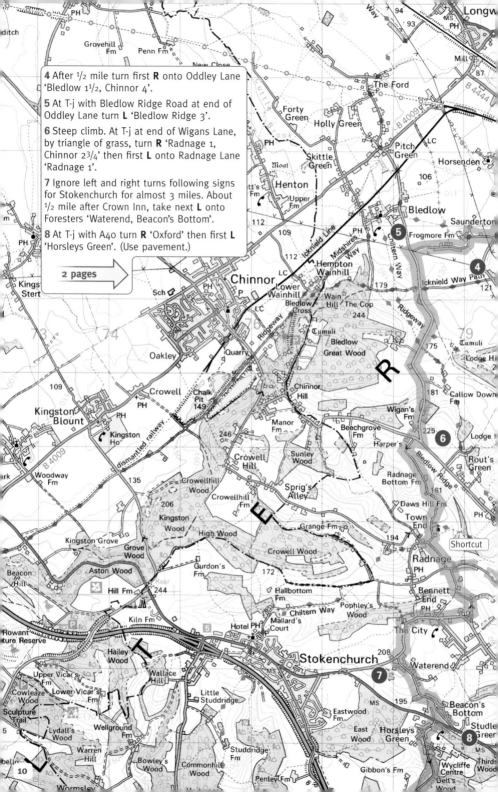

4 After ½ mile turn first **R** onto Oddley Lane 'Bledlow 1½, Chinnor 4'.

5 At T-j with Bledlow Ridge Road at end of Oddley Lane turn **L** 'Bledlow Ridge 3'.

6 Steep climb. At T-j at end of Wigans Lane, by triangle of grass, turn **R** 'Radnage 1, Chinnor 2¾' then first **L** onto Radnage Lane 'Radnage 1'.

7 Ignore left and right turns following signs for Stokenchurch for almost 3 miles. About ½ mile after Crown Inn, take next **L** onto Foresters 'Waterend, Beacon's Bottom'.

8 At T-j with A40 turn **R** 'Oxford' then first **L** 'Horsleys Green'. (Use pavement.)

2 pages

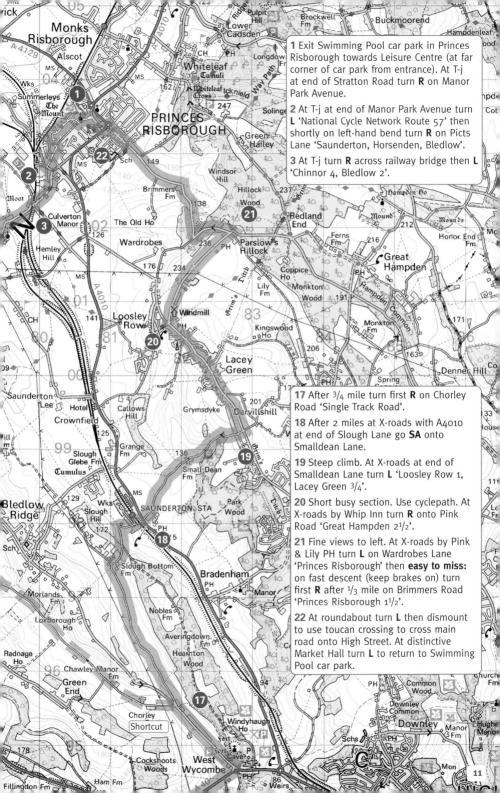

1 Exit Swimming Pool car park in Princes Risborough towards Leisure Centre (at far corner of car park from entrance). At T-j at end of Stratton Road turn **R** on Manor Park Avenue.

2 At T-j at end of Manor Park Avenue turn **L** 'National Cycle Network Route 57' then shortly on left-hand bend turn **R** on Picts Lane 'Saunderton, Horsenden, Bledlow'.

3 At T-j turn **R** across railway bridge then **L** 'Chinnor 4, Bledlow 2'.

17 After 3/4 mile turn first **R** on Chorley Road 'Single Track Road'.

18 After 2 miles at X-roads with A4010 at end of Slough Lane go **SA** onto Smalldean Lane.

19 Steep climb. At X-roads at end of Smalldean Lane turn **L** 'Loosley Row 1, Lacey Green 3/4'.

20 Short busy section. Use cyclepath. At X-roads by Whip Inn turn **R** onto Pink Road 'Great Hampden 2½'.

21 Fine views to left. At X-roads by Pink & Lily PH turn **L** on Wardrobes Lane 'Princes Risborough' then **easy to miss:** on fast descent (keep brakes on) turn first **R** after 1/3 mile on Brimmers Road 'Princes Risborough 1½'.

22 At roundabout turn **L** then dismount to use toucan crossing to cross main road onto High Street. At distinctive Market Hall turn **L** to return to Swimming Pool car park.

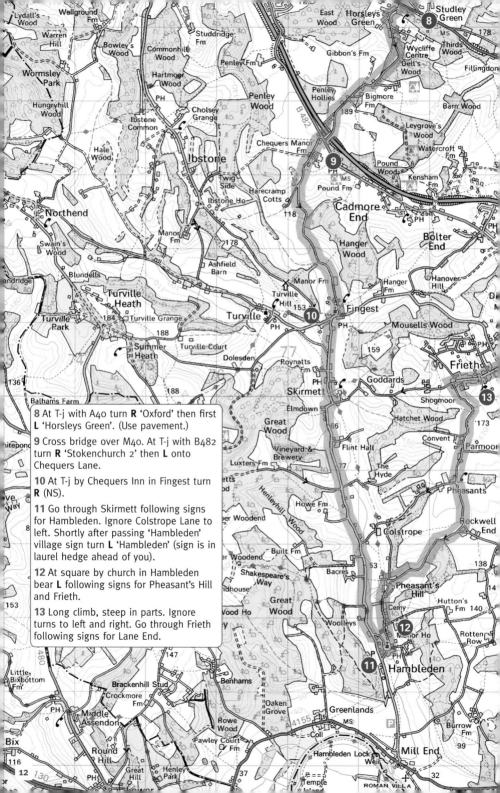

8 At T-j with A40 turn **R** 'Oxford' then first **L** 'Horsleys Green'. (Use pavement.)

9 Cross bridge over M40. At T-j with B482 turn **R** 'Stokenchurch 2' then **L** onto Chequers Lane.

10 At T-j by Chequers Inn in Fingest turn **R** (NS).

11 Go through Skirmett following signs for Hambleden. Ignore Colstrope Lane to left. Shortly after passing 'Hambleden' village sign turn **L** 'Hambleden' (sign is in laurel hedge ahead of you).

12 At square by church in Hambleden bear **L** following signs for Pheasant's Hill and Frieth.

13 Long climb, steep in parts. Ignore turns to left and right. Go through Frieth following signs for Lane End.

14 In Lane End, at T-j with B482, turn **R** then **L** 'Wheeler End 1½, High Wycombe 6'.

15 On sharp right-hand bend after ⅓ mile, turn **L** on Bullocks Farm Lane 'Wheeler End ½, West Wycombe 2½'.

16 Steep descent. At T-j with A40 turn **R** (NS). Use cycleway. Turn first **L** 'Bledlow Ridge 3'.

← 2 pages

Through the Chilterns from Chesham to Tring

O n the map, Chesham appears to be at the centre of a spider's web of roads and lanes with no fewer than 14 of them radiating out from the central point. However, less than a mile after the start you are into the countryside on a network of quiet lanes that climb through attractive farmland and beechwoods to a high point at Hastoe, on the Ridgeway. Lose all your height as you plunge down off the escarpment into the attractive town of

Tring, with its nearby nature reserves. The town is located at a low point in the Chiltern Hills known as the Tring Gap which has been used as a crossing point since ancient times - the Icknield Way links the Ridgeway to the flint mines at Grimes Graves on the Norfolk / Suffolk border; Akeman Street was the Roman Road linking London to Cirencester. More recently the gap has been used for the Grand Union Canal and the railway. The climb up from Tring is steep and there is a particularly tough section just

before the radio mast at the top of the hill. Once back on top of the Chiltern escarpment the ride is a rollercoaster of several shorter climbs and descents, much of it through fine beechwoods before the final swoop back down into Chesham.

NB To avoid traffic on the exit from Chesham the route uses a $^1/_2$ mile section of stone track (Instruction 5). You may prefer to walk this bit or alternatively use the direct (busier) road to Asheridge from the centre of Chesham.

Overview

On-road ● 24 miles / 39 kilometres ● Strenuous

Start
Clock Tower / Red Lion PH in the centre of Chesham

Parking
Follow signs

Busy roads
None

Terrain
Hilly. The first climb, from Chesham to Hastoe, above Tring, is the longest. The second starts in Tring with a very steep section up to the mast at the summit **10**

Nearest railway
Chesham or Tring

Refreshments

Chesham
Lots of choice

Asheridge
Blue Ball PH
T: 01494 758263

Cholesbury
Full Moon PH
T: 01494 758959

Tring
Lots of choice

Lee Gate
Old Swan PH
T: 01494 837239
The Gate Inn
T: 01494 837368

Map pages

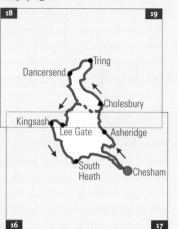

Other rides nearby

Ride 2

Ride 3
Page 20

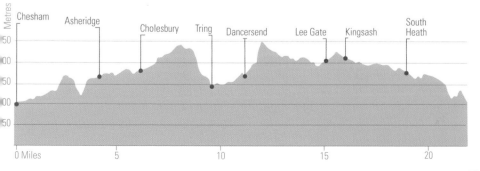

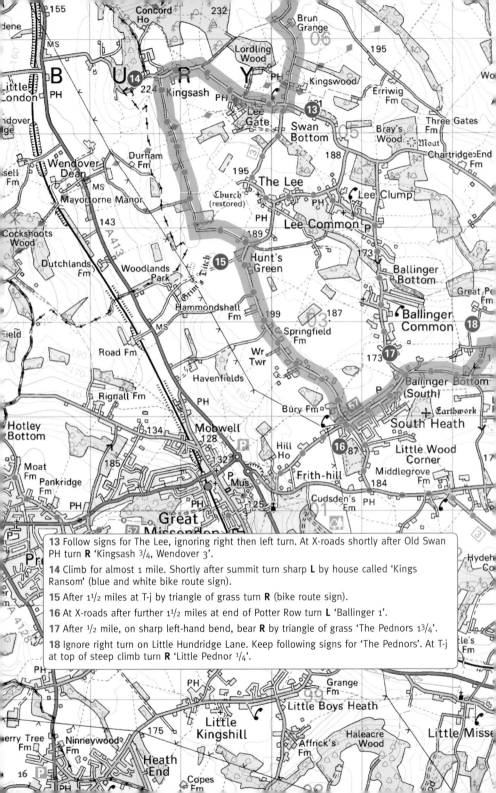

13 Follow signs for The Lee, ignoring right then left turn. At X-roads shortly after Old Swan PH turn **R** 'Kingsash 3/4, Wendover 3'.

14 Climb for almost 1 mile. Shortly after summit turn sharp **L** by house called 'Kings Ransom' (blue and white bike route sign).

15 After 1 1/2 miles at T-j by triangle of grass turn **R** (bike route sign).

16 At X-roads after further 1 1/2 miles at end of Potter Row turn **L** 'Ballinger 1'.

17 After 1/2 mile, on sharp left-hand bend, bear **R** by triangle of grass 'The Pednors 1 3/4'.

18 Ignore right turn on Little Hundridge Lane. Keep following signs for 'The Pednors'. At T-j at top of steep climb turn **R** 'Little Pednor 1/4'.

1 From clocktower in centre of Chesham cross via toucan crossing towards Red Lion PH onto Germain Street. Ignore turns to right and left and follow road round to **R** as it becomes Wey Lane.

2 At offset X-roads by Queen's Head PH turn **R** then **L** on Church Lane. Shortly bear **L** then after 400yds at fork bear **R** following signs for 'Pednor Bottom, Single Track Road'.

3 Easy to miss: after 1¾ miles and soon after horse training area on right, take first **R** uphill on West Dean Lane.

4 At T-j at top of West Dean Lane turn **R** then ignore first left on Old Sax Lane. **Easy to miss:** after ⅓ mile, immediately after house number '363' on left, opposite red-brick wall on right, take next **L** downhill on Buslins Lane 'Bridleway'.

5 Follow lane / stone track downhill then around right and left hand bends. After ½ mile at T-j with road opposite Hazeldene Farm turn **L**.

2 pages →

19 After 2¼ miles at T-j at end of Drydell Lane turn **R** 'Chesham' to rejoin outward route: at T-j at end of Pednor Road turn **R** then **L** by Queen's Head PH onto Wey Lane. Ignore right and left turns to return to clocktower.

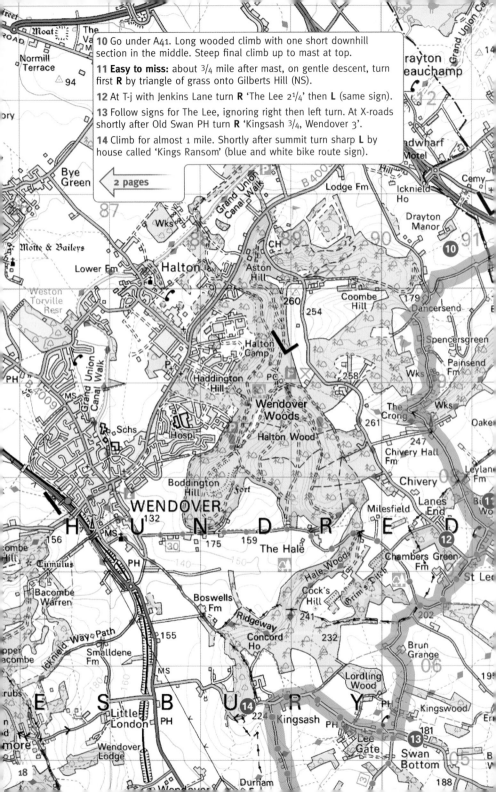

10 Go under A41. Long wooded climb with one short downhill section in the middle. Steep final climb up to mast at top.

11 **Easy to miss:** about 3/4 mile after mast, on gentle descent, turn first **R** by triangle of grass onto Gilberts Hill (NS).

12 At T-j with Jenkins Lane turn **R** 'The Lee 2¼' then **L** (same sign).

13 Follow signs for The Lee, ignoring right then left turn. At X-roads shortly after Old Swan PH turn **R** 'Kingsash 3/4, Wendover 3'.

14 Climb for almost 1 mile. Shortly after summit turn sharp **L** by house called 'Kings Ransom' (blue and white bike route sign).

2 pages

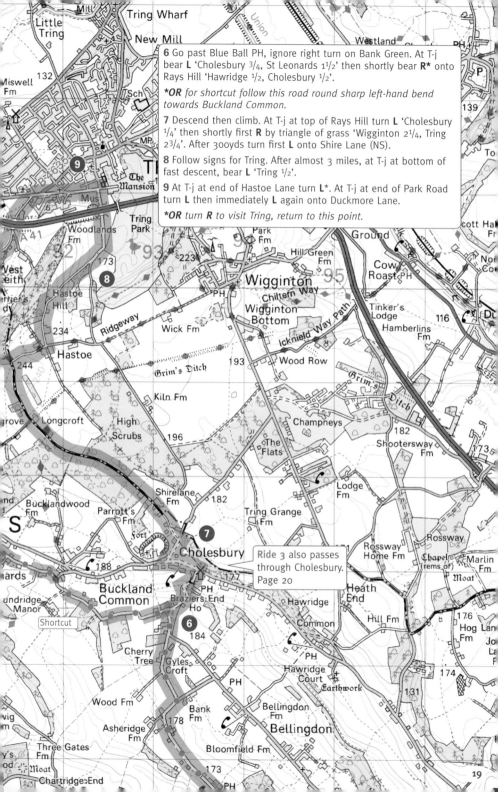

6 Go past Blue Ball PH, ignore right turn on Bank Green. At T-j bear **L** 'Cholesbury ³/₄, St Leonards 1¹/₂' then shortly bear **R*** onto Rays Hill 'Hawridge ¹/₂, Cholesbury ¹/₂'.

***OR** for shortcut follow this road round sharp left-hand bend towards Buckland Common.*

7 Descend then climb. At T-j at top of Rays Hill turn **L** 'Cholesbury ¹/₄' then shortly first **R** by triangle of grass 'Wigginton 2¹/₄, Tring 2³/₄'. After 300yds turn first **L** onto Shire Lane (NS).

8 Follow signs for Tring. After almost 3 miles, at T-j at bottom of fast descent, bear **L** 'Tring ¹/₂'.

9 At T-j at end of Hastoe Lane turn **L***. At T-j at end of Park Road turn **L** then immediately **L** again onto Duckmore Lane.

***OR** turn **R** to visit Tring, return to this point.*

Ride 3 also passes through Cholesbury. Page 20

Shortcut

19

Tring along the canal to Hemel Hempstead & into the wooded hills around Cholesbury

The towpath of the Grand Union Canal offers a scenic, flat and traffic-free option southeast from Tring to Hemel Hempstead, avoiding the busy roads through Berkhamsted. The price to pay for this is that the first ½ mile off-road, as far as Cow Roast Lock, is quite rough. Along its whole length the towpath should be taken at a leisurely pace as there are often people out walking, especially through the centre of Berkhamsted. Unique among English canals in being composed of eight separate canals, the Grand Union Canal links London with Birmingham, Leicester and Nottingham. Up to the 1920s all these canals were owned by quite separate companies. In 1929 the whole system was integrated as the Grand Union Canal. Having left the towpath at the southern end of Hemel Hempstead the ride explores the dense network of lanes criss-crossing the countryside west towards Chesham, with two good pub options in Flaunden or by the windmill in Cholesbury.

NB This ride features a long section on canal towpath with a short rough section at the start. It is passable on most bikes other than lightweight road bikes. Best to use 28-35mm tyres on road bikes or mountain bikes with slick tyres.

Overview
On-road ● 29 miles / 47 kilometres ● Moderate

Start
Car park at east end of Tring
High Street

Parking
As above

Busy roads
The road south from Tring
Station to the start of the canal
towpath **2** to **3**

Terrain
Two main climbs: the first
starts as soon as you leave the
canal towpath up to Bulstrode.
The second is longer, starting
from Flaunden Bottom and
reaching the ride's highest
point near Hastoe, above Tring

Nearest railway
Tring

Other rides nearby

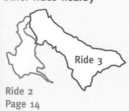

Ride 3

Ride 2
Page 14

Refreshments
Tring
Lots of choice

Berkhamsted
Lots of choice

Hemel Hempstead
Lots of choice

Flaunden
Bricklayers Arms PH
T: 01442 833322
Green Dragon PH
T: 01442 832269

Botley
Crown PH
T: 01494 783910

Cholesbury
Full Moon PH
T: 01494 758959

Map pages

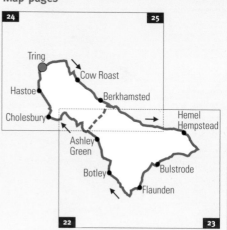

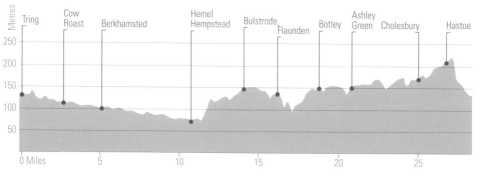

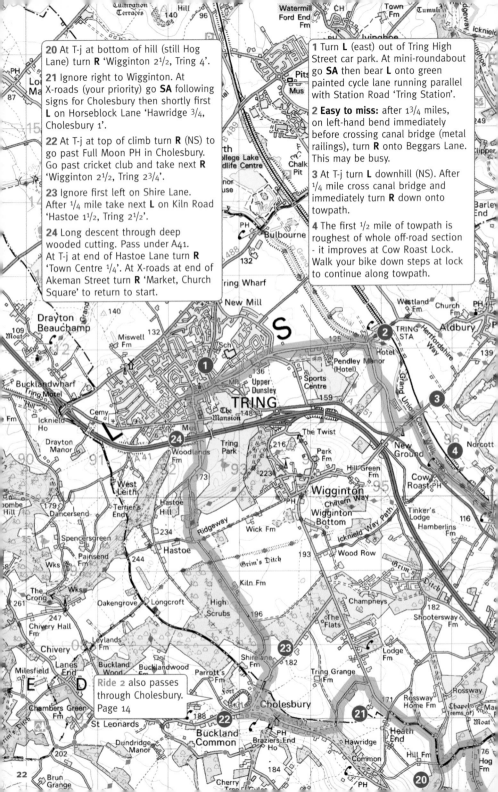

20 At T-j at bottom of hill (still Hog Lane) turn **R** 'Wigginton 2½, Tring 4'.

21 Ignore right to Wigginton. At X-roads (your priority) go **SA** following signs for Cholesbury then shortly first **L** on Horseblock Lane 'Hawridge ¾, Cholesbury 1'.

22 At T-j at top of climb turn **R** (NS) to go past Full Moon PH in Cholesbury. Go past cricket club and take next **R** 'Wigginton 2½, Tring 2¾'.

23 Ignore first left on Shire Lane. After ¼ mile take next **L** on Kiln Road 'Hastoe 1½, Tring 2½'.

24 Long descent through deep wooded cutting. Pass under A41. At T-j at end of Hastoe Lane turn **R** 'Town Centre ¼'. At X-roads at end of Akeman Street turn **R** 'Market, Church Square' to return to start.

1 Turn **L** (east) out of Tring High Street car park. At mini-roundabout go **SA** then bear **L** onto green painted cycle lane running parallel with Station Road 'Tring Station'.

2 Easy to miss: after 1¾ miles, on left-hand bend immediately before crossing canal bridge (metal railings), turn **R** onto Beggars Lane. This may be busy.

3 At T-j turn **L** downhill (NS). After ¼ mile cross canal bridge and immediately turn **R** down onto towpath.

4 The first ½ mile of towpath is roughest of whole off-road section - it improves at Cow Roast Lock. Walk your bike down steps at lock to continue along towpath.

Ride 2 also passes through Cholesbury. Page 14

5 Towpath crosses sides several times. Go through Berkhamsted and follow towpath on variety of surfaces for further 6 miles into Hemel Hempstead, past Apsley Marina and Woody's Cafe.

2 pages

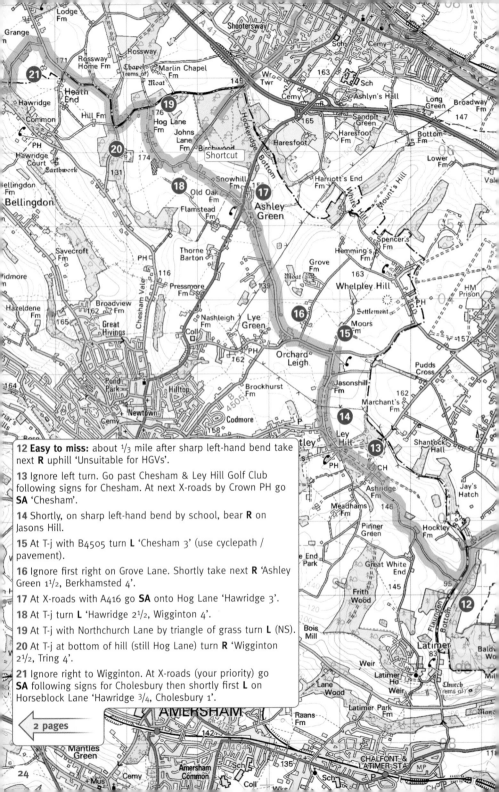

12 Easy to miss: about ⅓ mile after sharp left-hand bend take next **R** uphill 'Unsuitable for HGVs'.

13 Ignore left turn. Go past Chesham & Ley Hill Golf Club following signs for Chesham. At next X-roads by Crown PH go **SA** 'Chesham'.

14 Shortly, on sharp left-hand bend by school, bear **R** on Jasons Hill.

15 At T-j with B4505 turn **L** 'Chesham 3' (use cyclepath / pavement).

16 Ignore first right on Grove Lane. Shortly take next **R** 'Ashley Green 1½, Berkhamsted 4'.

17 At X-roads with A416 go **SA** onto Hog Lane 'Hawridge 3'.

18 At T-j turn **L** 'Hawridge 2½, Wigginton 4'.

19 At T-j with Northchurch Lane by triangle of grass turn **L** (NS).

20 At T-j at bottom of hill (still Hog Lane) turn **R** 'Wigginton 2½, Tring 4'.

21 Ignore right to Wigginton. At X-roads (your priority) go **SA** following signs for Cholesbury then shortly first **L** on Horseblock Lane 'Hawridge ¾, Cholesbury 1'.

2 pages

24

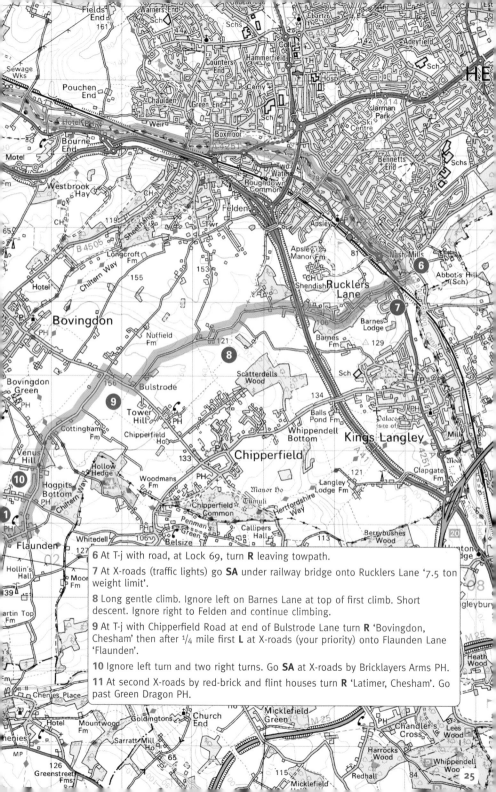

6 At T-j with road, at Lock 69, turn **R** leaving towpath.

7 At X-roads (traffic lights) go **SA** under railway bridge onto Rucklers Lane '7.5 ton weight limit'.

8 Long gentle climb. Ignore left on Barnes Lane at top of first climb. Short descent. Ignore right to Felden and continue climbing.

9 At T-j with Chipperfield Road at end of Bulstrode Lane turn **R** 'Bovingdon, Chesham' then after ¼ mile first **L** at X-roads (your priority) onto Flaunden Lane 'Flaunden'.

10 Ignore left turn and two right turns. Go **SA** at X-roads by Bricklayers Arms PH.

11 At second X-roads by red-brick and flint houses turn **R** 'Latimer, Chesham'. Go past Green Dragon PH.

25

South of Hitchin to Ayot St Lawrence

A combination of back streets and a subway gives the quickest exit from the centre of Hitchin out into the countryside and the network of quiet lanes. The ride weaves its way through arable fields and clumps of broadleaf woodland, with the odd incongruous aircraft disturbing the peace, as the route passes within a couple of miles of Luton airport. A series of sneaky right and left turns avoids the built-up areas of Harpenden and

Wheathampstead, twice crossing the River Lea as it makes its way east from Luton to Hertford then south to London. The proximity of the old Roman settlement of Verulamium at St Albans manifests itself in the dead straight Roman Road running through Coleman Green. The next highlight is Shaw's Corner at Ayot St Lawrence, a peaceful village where George Bernard Shaw made his home, scarcely altered since his death in 1950. Also of note in the village are the ruined 14th-century church and its 18th-century Grecian-style successor, a series of timber-framed cottages and the 17th century Old Rectory. From Ayot St Lawrence the ride wiggles its way north to Charlton to rejoin the outward route and use the same quiet streets and the subway beneath the busy A602 back into the centre of Hitchin.

NB Do not fall off your bike in surprise if you spot black squirrels on this ride - the area is renowned for them!

Overview

On-road ● 32 miles / 50 kilometres ● Moderate

Start
Market Place, Hitchin

Parking
Several town centre car parks
- follow signs

Busy road
None

Terrain
Undulating

Nearest railway
Hitchin

Other rides nearby

Ride 5
Page 32

Ride 4

Refreshments
Hitchin
Lots of choice

Charlton
Windmill PH
T: 01462 432096

Peters Green
Bright Star PH
T: 01438 832351

Amwell
Elephant & Castle PH
T: 01582 832175

Coleman Green
John Bunyan PH
T: 01582 832037

Ayot St Lawrence
Brocket Arms PH
T: 01438 820250

Gosmore
Bull PH
T: 01462 440035
Bird in Hand PH
T: 01462 432079

Map pages

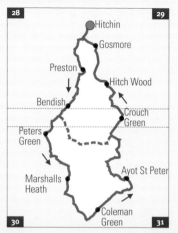

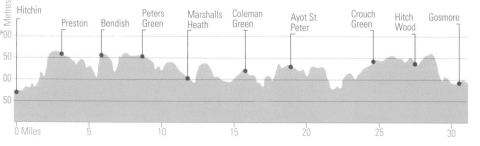

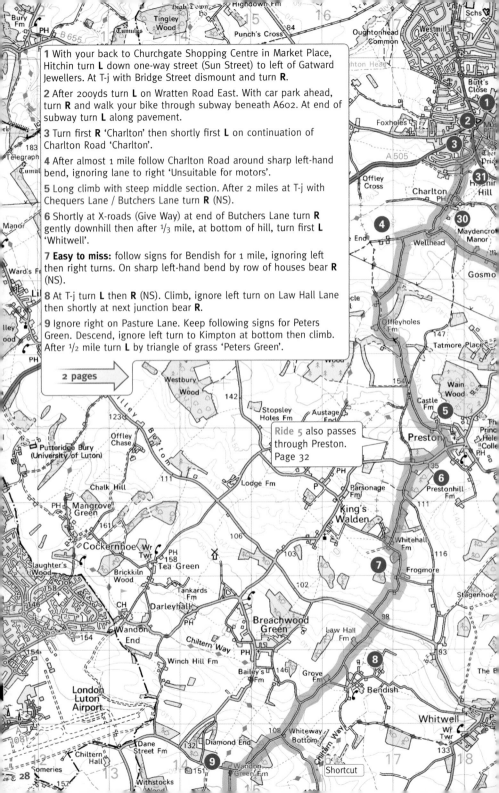

1 With your back to Churchgate Shopping Centre in Market Place, Hitchin turn **L** down one-way street (Sun Street) to left of Gatward Jewellers. At T-j with Bridge Street dismount and turn **R**.

2 After 200yds turn **L** on Wratten Road East. With car park ahead, turn **R** and walk your bike through subway beneath A602. At end of subway turn **L** along pavement.

3 Turn first **R** 'Charlton' then shortly first **L** on continuation of Charlton Road 'Charlton'.

4 After almost 1 mile follow Charlton Road around sharp left-hand bend, ignoring lane to right 'Unsuitable for motors'.

5 Long climb with steep middle section. After 2 miles at T-j with Chequers Lane / Butchers Lane turn **R** (NS).

6 Shortly at X-roads (Give Way) at end of Butchers Lane turn **R** gently downhill then after 1/3 mile, at bottom of hill, turn first **L** 'Whitwell'.

7 Easy to miss: follow signs for Bendish for 1 mile, ignoring left then right turns. On sharp left-hand bend by row of houses bear **R** (NS).

8 At T-j turn **L** then **R** (NS). Climb, ignore left turn on Law Hall Lane then shortly at next junction bear **R**.

9 Ignore right on Pasture Lane. Keep following signs for Peters Green. Descend, ignore left turn to Kimpton at bottom then climb. After 1/2 mile turn **L** by triangle of grass 'Peters Green'.

2 pages

Ride 5 also passes through Preston. Page 32

Shortcut

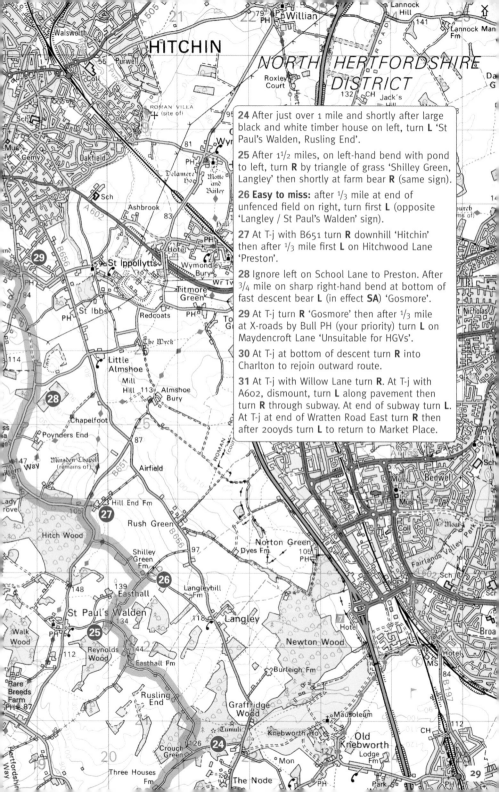

24 After just over 1 mile and shortly after large black and white timber house on left, turn **L** 'St Paul's Walden, Rusling End'.

25 After 1½ miles, on left-hand bend with pond to left, turn **R** by triangle of grass 'Shilley Green, Langley' then shortly at farm bear **R** (same sign).

26 Easy to miss: after ⅓ mile at end of unfenced field on right, turn first **L** (opposite 'Langley / St Paul's Walden' sign).

27 At T-j with B651 turn **R** downhill 'Hitchin' then after ⅓ mile first **L** on Hitchwood Lane 'Preston'.

28 Ignore left on School Lane to Preston. After ¾ mile on sharp right-hand bend at bottom of fast descent bear **L** (in effect **SA**) 'Gosmore'.

29 At T-j turn **R** 'Gosmore' then after ⅓ mile at X-roads by Bull PH (your priority) turn **L** on Maydencroft Lane 'Unsuitable for HGVs'.

30 At T-j at bottom of descent turn **R** into Charlton to rejoin outward route.

31 At T-j with Willow Lane turn **R**. At T-j with A602, dismount, turn **L** along pavement then turn **R** through subway. At end of subway turn **L**. At T-j at end of Wratten Road East turn **R** then after 200yds turn **L** to return to Market Place.

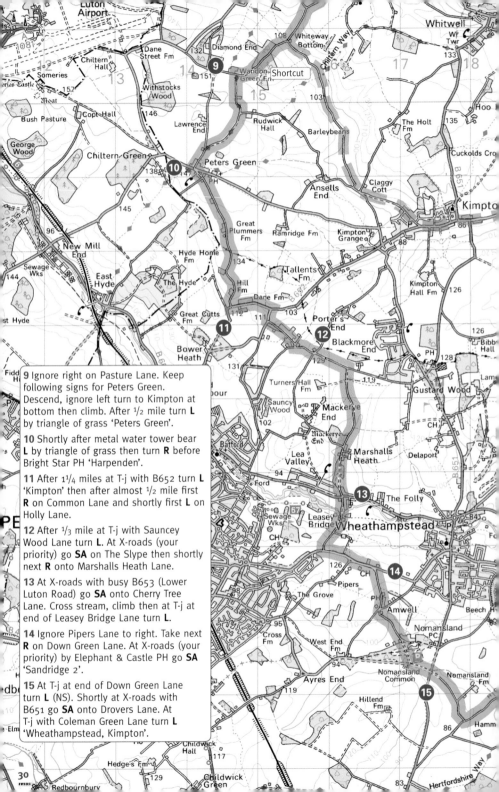

9 Ignore right on Pasture Lane. Keep following signs for Peters Green. Descend, ignore left turn to Kimpton at bottom then climb. After ½ mile turn **L** by triangle of grass 'Peters Green'.

10 Shortly after metal water tower bear **L** by triangle of grass then turn **R** before Bright Star PH 'Harpenden'.

11 After 1¼ miles at T-j with B652 turn **L** 'Kimpton' then after almost ½ mile first **R** on Common Lane and shortly first **L** on Holly Lane.

12 After ⅓ mile at T-j with Sauncey Wood Lane turn **L**. At X-roads (your priority) go **SA** on The Slype then shortly next **R** onto Marshalls Heath Lane.

13 At X-roads with busy B653 (Lower Luton Road) go **SA** onto Cherry Tree Lane. Cross stream, climb then at T-j at end of Leasey Bridge Lane turn **L**.

14 Ignore Pipers Lane to right. Take next **R** on Down Green Lane. At X-roads (your priority) by Elephant & Castle PH go **SA** 'Sandridge 2'.

15 At T-j at end of Down Green Lane turn **L** (NS). Shortly at X-roads with B651 go **SA** onto Drovers Lane. At T-j with Coleman Green Lane turn **L** 'Wheathampstead, Kimpton'.

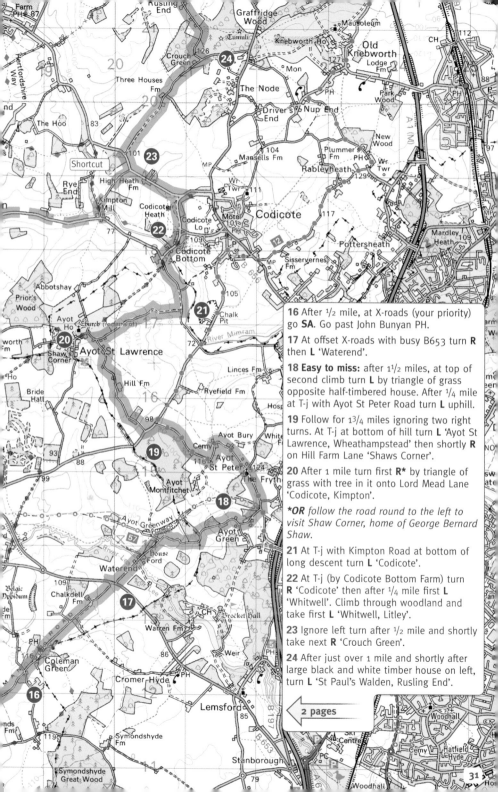

16 After ½ mile, at X-roads (your priority) go **SA**. Go past John Bunyan PH.

17 At offset X-roads with busy B653 turn **R** then **L** 'Waterend'.

18 Easy to miss: after 1½ miles, at top of second climb turn **L** by triangle of grass opposite half-timbered house. After ¼ mile at T-j with Ayot St Peter Road turn **L** uphill.

19 Follow for 1¾ miles ignoring two right turns. At T-j at bottom of hill turn **L** 'Ayot St Lawrence, Wheathampstead' then shortly **R** on Hill Farm Lane 'Shaws Corner'.

20 After 1 mile turn first **R*** by triangle of grass with tree in it onto Lord Mead Lane 'Codicote, Kimpton'.

*OR *follow the road round to the left to visit Shaw Corner, home of George Bernard Shaw.*

21 At T-j with Kimpton Road at bottom of long descent turn **L** 'Codicote'.

22 At T-j (by Codicote Bottom Farm) turn **R** 'Codicote' then after ¼ mile first **L** 'Whitwell'. Climb through woodland and take first **L** 'Whitwell, Litley'.

23 Ignore left turn after ½ mile and shortly take next **R** 'Crouch Green'.

24 After just over 1 mile and shortly after large black and white timber house on left, turn **L** 'St Paul's Walden, Rusling End'.

2 pages

A ring around Stevenage from Codicote

This ride appears to defy logic: all around are large centres of population such as Stevenage, Hitchin, Welwyn Garden City and Luton, and yet a good part of the ride is spent on lanes where you are as likely to see pheasants as cars. There is a small price to pay for this: a plethora of instructions are needed to keep you away from the busy roads and lanes and on the quieter ones. It is a ride that improves each time you ride it as you need to spend less time looking at the instructions. The route passes through some lovely woodland and there are several fine views along the way. About one third of the way around the ride you pass Benington Lordship Gardens, hill-top gardens designed around the 18th-century manor house. There are rock and water gardens, a walled kitchen garden and a magnificent display of roses. A little further on, Walkern's claim to fame is that it was here in 1711 that the trial of Jane Wenham took place, the last person to be condemned to death for witchcraft in England. She was accused, among other things, of bewitching sheep to death and appearing in the guise of a cat! The culture stop is at the end: the house of George Bernard Shaw at Ayot St Lawrence.

Overview

On-road ● 35 miles / 56 kilometres ● Moderate

Start
The Goat PH, High Street, Codicote, 5 miles south of Stevenage

Parking
No specific parking. Park in the High Street, showing consideration

Busy roads
● The A602 is used for ¼ mile east of Stevenage - there is a (narrow) pavement **6**

● Some busier roads in the Graveley / Great Wymondley / St Ippollytts area **14** to **17**

Terrain
Undulating with several climbs of 100-200ft

Nearest railway
Knebworth or Watton at Stone

Refreshments
Codicote
Lots of choice

Benington
Bell PH
T: 01438 869270

Walkern
White Lion PH
T: 01438 861251

Graveley
George & Dragon PH
T: 01438 351362
Waggon & Horses PH
T: 01438 367658

Great Wymondley
Green Man PH
T: 01438 357217

Preston
Red Lion PH
T: 01462 459585

Gustard Wood
Cross Keys PH
T: 01582 832165

Ayot St Lawrence
Brocket Arms PH
T: 01438 820250

Other rides nearby

Map pages

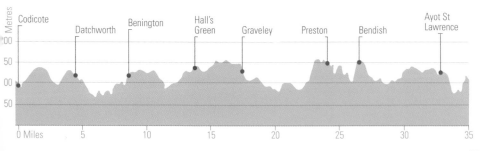

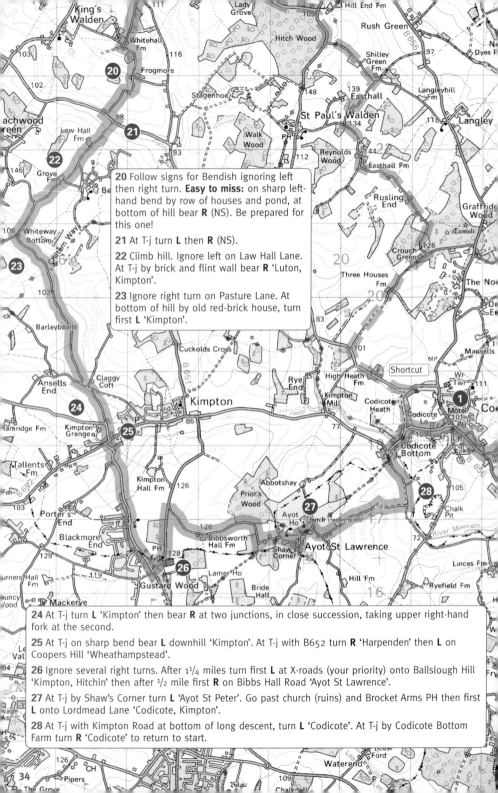

20 Follow signs for Bendish ignoring left then right turn. **Easy to miss:** on sharp left-hand bend by row of houses and pond, at bottom of hill bear **R** (NS). Be prepared for this one!

21 At T-j turn **L** then **R** (NS).

22 Climb hill. Ignore left on Law Hall Lane. At T-j by brick and flint wall bear **R** 'Luton, Kimpton'.

23 Ignore right turn on Pasture Lane. At bottom of hill by old red-brick house, turn first **L** 'Kimpton'.

24 At T-j turn **L** 'Kimpton' then bear **R** at two junctions, in close succession, taking upper right-hand fork at the second.

25 At T-j on sharp bend bear **L** downhill 'Kimpton'. At T-j with B652 turn **R** 'Harpenden' then **L** on Coopers Hill 'Wheathampstead'.

26 Ignore several right turns. After 1¼ miles turn first **L** at X-roads (your priority) onto Ballslough Hill 'Kimpton, Hitchin' then after ½ mile first **R** on Bibbs Hall Road 'Ayot St Lawrence'.

27 At T-j by Shaw's Corner turn **L** 'Ayot St Peter'. Go past church (ruins) and Brocket Arms PH then first **L** onto Lordmead Lane 'Codicote, Kimpton'.

28 At T-j with Kimpton Road at bottom of long descent, turn **L** 'Codicote'. At T-j by Codicote Bottom Farm turn **R** 'Codicote' to return to start.

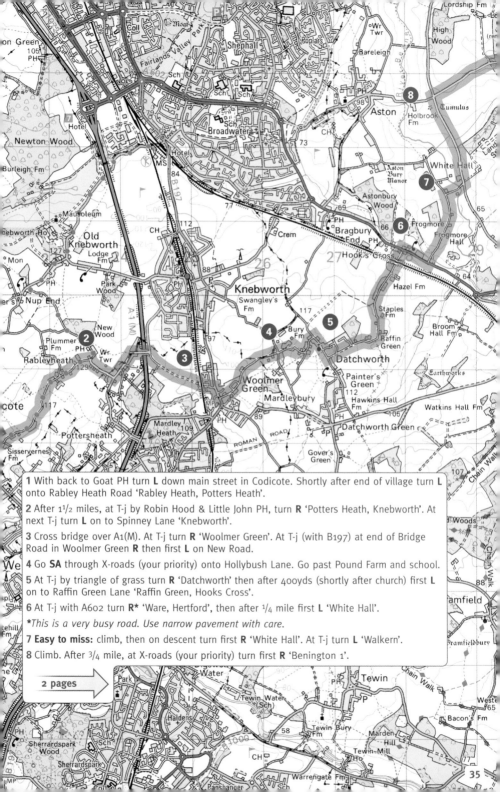

1 With back to Goat PH turn **L** down main street in Codicote. Shortly after end of village turn **L** onto Rabley Heath Road 'Rabley Heath, Potters Heath'.

2 After 1½ miles, at T-j by Robin Hood & Little John PH, turn **R** 'Potters Heath, Knebworth'. At next T-j turn **L** on to Spinney Lane 'Knebworth'.

3 Cross bridge over A1(M). At T-j turn **R** 'Woolmer Green'. At T-j (with B197) at end of Bridge Road in Woolmer Green **R** then first **L** on New Road.

4 Go **SA** through X-roads (your priority) onto Hollybush Lane. Go past Pound Farm and school.

5 At T-j by triangle of grass turn **R** 'Datchworth' then after 400yds (shortly after church) first **L** on to Raffin Green Lane 'Raffin Green, Hooks Cross'.

6 At T-j with A602 turn **R*** 'Ware, Hertford', then after ¼ mile first **L** 'White Hall'.

This is a very busy road. Use narrow pavement with care.

7 Easy to miss: climb, then on descent turn first **R** 'White Hall'. At T-j turn **L** 'Walkern'.

8 Climb. After ¾ mile, at X-roads (your priority) turn first **R** 'Benington 1'.

2 pages ➡

14 Follow this road for 2½ miles, ignoring turns and descending steeply. At T-j (with B197) in Graveley at end of Church Lane turn **R** (busier) then after ¼ mile first **L** 'Great Wymondley'.

15 At T-j at end of Graveley Lane turn **R** 'Great Wymondley' then on right-hand bend by Green Man PH, bear **L** 'Stevenage 3'.

16 At roundabout go **SA** on to Blakemere End Road 'Titmore Green' (may be busy). At T-j in Redcoats turn **R** 'St Ippollytts ¾' then first **L** 'Preston, Little Almshoe'.

17 At X-roads with B656 go **SA** 'Preston'.

18 After 1¼ miles at top of hill, turn **R** on School Lane 'Preston'. At village green in Preston by Red Lion PH take second **L** onto Church Lane 'King's Walden, Breachwood Green'.

19 Ignore first left at X-roads after 400yds. Take next **L** 'Whitwell'.

← 2 pages

Ride 4 also passes through Preston. Page 26

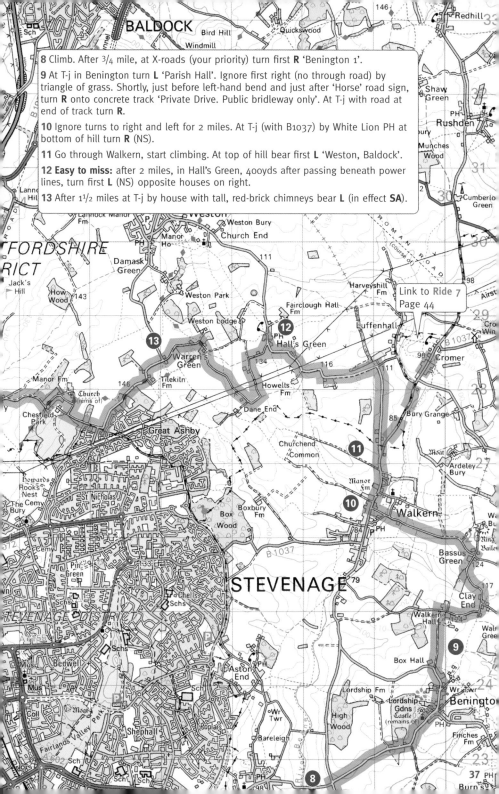

8 Climb. After 3/4 mile, at X-roads (your priority) turn first **R** 'Benington 1'.

9 At T-j in Benington turn **L** 'Parish Hall'. Ignore first right (no through road) by triangle of grass. Shortly, just before left-hand bend and just after 'Horse' road sign, turn **R** onto concrete track 'Private Drive. Public bridleway only'. At T-j with road at end of track turn **R**.

10 Ignore turns to right and left for 2 miles. At T-j (with B1037) by White Lion PH at bottom of hill turn **R** (NS).

11 Go through Walkern, start climbing. At top of hill bear first **L** 'Weston, Baldock'.

12 Easy to miss: after 2 miles, in Hall's Green, 400yds after passing beneath power lines, turn first **L** (NS) opposite houses on right.

13 After 1½ miles at T-j by house with tall, red-brick chimneys bear **L** (in effect **SA**).

Link to Ride 7
Page 44

The Lee Navigation from Hertford to London

This superb open section of canal towpath is one of the best in the region. The whole Lee Valley has become one of the finest areas for recreational cycling to the north of London. The ride described here follows the Lee Navigation from its northern terminus in Hertford eastwards through the attractive town of Ware before taking a southerly course through to Waltham Abbey and all the way into London, joining the Thames near Limehouse Basin. To look at the map one would imagine seeing a succession of vast reservoirs along the valley. As

it is, the towpath lies below the embankments surrounding the reservoirs and they remain hidden. There are lot of pubs and a couple of cafés along the way so you have plenty of reasons for taking this ride at a leisurely pace. At the southern end there are several canals: the Regents Canal which emerges from Islington Tunnel is part of the Grand Union Canal, leading to its junction with the Thames at Limehouse Basin; the Hertford Union Canal links Regents Canal with the Lee Navigation alongside Victoria Park and then there is the Limehouse Cut.

NB This ride is unlike all the others in the book: for a start it is a linear ride which means it can be as short or as long as you want, or you can ride it one way and catch the train back. Secondly it is neither a road ride (it is all on a fine gravel towpath) nor a mountain bike ride as it is completely flat.

Overview

On-road ● 28 miles (one way) / 45 kilometres ● Easy

Start & Parking

● **Hertford.** The Swimming Pool / Leisure Centre on Hartham Lane, Hertford. From the centre of Hertford follow signs for the B158 (Parliament Square roundabout, The Wash, Millbridge) past the library then turn right onto Hartham Lane past Hertford Brewery to the car park. The car park is free at the weekends

● **Waltham Abbey.** The best car parks for the canal towpath are signposted just to the north of the town, either at the Royal Gunpowder Mills (grid reference TL 377010) or a little way north along the B194 at Fishers Green (grid reference TL 376027). Another option is at Enfield Lock just south of the M25

● **Islington.** The west end of the tunnel at the junction of Noel Road, Danbury Street and Graham Street

Busy roads

● Care should be taken crossing the road in Ware - follow the signposted cycle crossing ❷

● There is another narrow but busy road to cross just south of Dobbs Weir ❸

Terrain

Flat

Nearest railway

Hertford or lots of choice all the way along the ride

Refreshments

Hertford
Lots of choice

Ware
Lots of choice

South of Ware
Jolly Fisherman PH
T: 01920 870125

Rye House
Rye House PH
T: 01992 465151

Dobb's Weir
Fish & Eels PH
T: 01992 466073

Waltham Abbey
Lots of choice

Tottenham
Water Edge Café at Stonebridge Lock

Upper Clapton
Springfield Park Café

Map pages

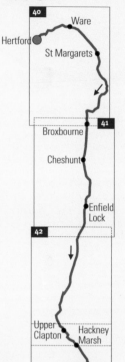

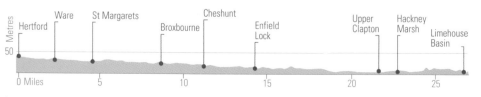

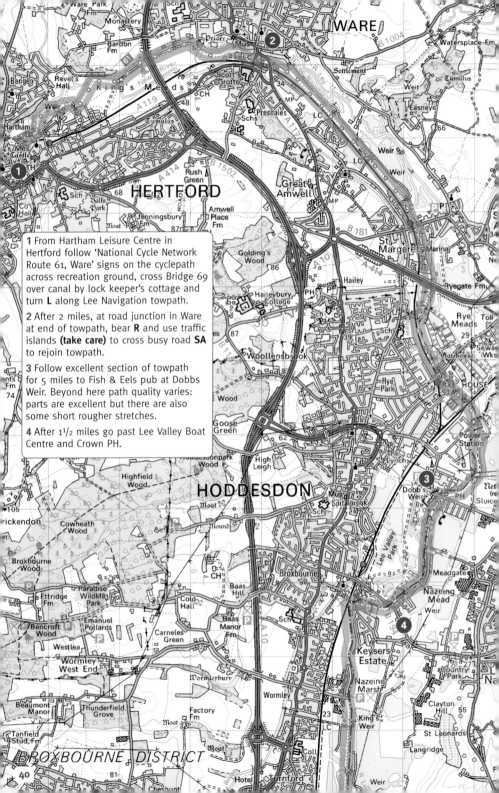

1 From Hartham Leisure Centre in Hertford follow 'National Cycle Network Route 61, Ware' signs on the cyclepath across recreation ground, cross Bridge 69 over canal by lock keeper's cottage and turn **L** along Lee Navigation towpath.

2 After 2 miles, at road junction in Ware at end of towpath, bear **R** and use traffic islands **(take care)** to cross busy road **SA** to rejoin towpath.

3 Follow excellent section of towpath for 5 miles to Fish & Eels pub at Dobbs Weir. Beyond here path quality varies: parts are excellent but there are also some short rougher stretches.

4 After 1½ miles go past Lee Valley Boat Centre and Crown PH.

5 Continue for 6 miles to Waltham Abbey (just after Waltham Town Lock, at Bridge 42).

6 Follow towpath south, with canal to your left. Pass under M25, go past Greyhound pub then Enfield Lock.

1 page →

7 After 6 miles go past Water Edge Café at Stonebridge Lock by Lee Valley Canoe & Cycle Centre.

8 After further 2 miles there is another café at north end of Springfield Park.

9 Go past hundreds of football fields that cover Hackney Marsh.

10 About 12 miles south of Waltham Abbey, and just south of Hackney Wick, you will need to turn off Lee Navigation onto Hertford Union Canal to continue south to Limehouse Basin or west to Islington on Regents Canal. This point is by the Olympic site, marked by a 3-way sign. Turn **R** 'Hertford Union, Victoria Park'.

11 Pass alongside Victoria Park then at T-j* with Regents Canal you can:

(a) turn **L** for 1½ miles to Limehouse Basin and River Thames

(b) turn **R** for 2½ miles for Islington, as far as tunnel (at junction of Noel Road, Danbury Street and Graham Street).

Remember this point for your return trip as it is easy to miss.

Link to Islington

North from Buntingford over rolling downland to Reed & Barkway

The downlands north of Buntingford are the highest point east of the Chilterns, rising to the lofty summit of 553ft (168m) at Therfield. Buntingford's attractive High Street must have been a nightmare before the bypass was built but it is now possible to appreciate its former glory as a staging post on the A10 north from London, located along the course of the old Roman Road of Ermine Street. South from Buntingford the ride explores little-used lanes through fine arable farmland, passing through a hamlet with the name of Nasty before turning westwards through Ardeley (the church is worth a visit for its carved wooden angels). Climb up through the villages of Roe Green, Sandon and Kelshall to the aforementioned dizzy heights at Therfield, with vast views out over the flat Cambridgeshire countryside. East from Therfield and Reed the ride visits Barkway, an attractive village of thatched cottages dating back to the 17th century and a Jacobean Manor Farm near to the 13th-century church. The village grew and prospered as a handy stopping place between Ware and Cambridge. The two tall milestones are part of what was probably the first example of regular milestone placing in Britain. Strike southwest past the golf course and Wyddial back to Buntingford.

Overview

On-road ● 29 miles / 47 kilometres ● Moderate

Start
Black Bull PH at the south end of the High Street, Buntingford

Parking
Free car park just off the High Street - follow signs

Busy roads
Very brief section on the A507 south of Rushden ⑧

Terrain
Undulating. The most noticeable climb is between Ardeley and Therfield

Nearest railway
Royston or Watton at Stone

Refreshments
Buntingford
Lots of choice

Westmill
Sword in Hand PH
T: 01763 271356

Ardeley
Jolly Waggoner PH
T: 01438 861350
Church Farm Café
T: 01438 861447

Rushden
Moon & Stars PH
T: 01763 288330

Therfield
Fox & Duck PH
T: 01763 287246

Barkway
Tally Ho PH
T: 01763 848389

Other rides nearby

Map pages

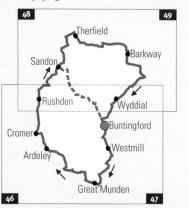

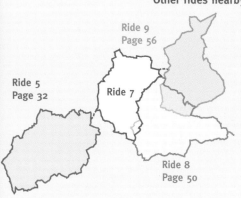

Ride 9
Page 56

Ride 5
Page 32

Ride 7

Ride 8
Page 50

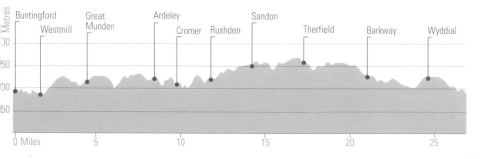

45

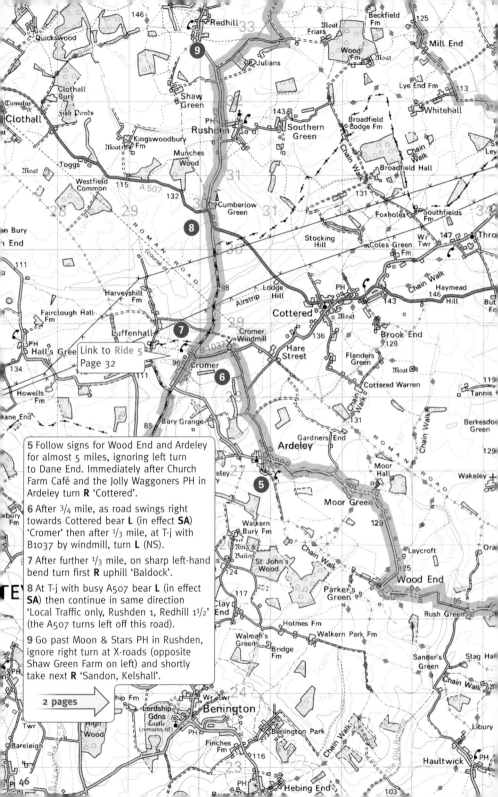

5 Follow signs for Wood End and Ardeley for almost 5 miles, ignoring left turn to Dane End. Immediately after Church Farm Café and the Jolly Waggoners PH in Ardeley turn **R** 'Cottered'.

6 After ³/₄ mile, as road swings right towards Cottered bear **L** (in effect **SA**) 'Cromer' then after ¹/₃ mile, at T-j with B1037 by windmill, turn **L** (NS).

7 After further ¹/₃ mile, on sharp left-hand bend turn first **R** uphill 'Baldock'.

8 At T-j with busy A507 bear **L** (in effect **SA**) then continue in same direction 'Local Traffic only, Rushden 1, Redhill 1¹/₂' (the A507 turns left off this road).

9 Go past Moon & Stars PH in Rushden, ignore right turn at X-roads (opposite Shaw Green Farm on left) and shortly take next **R** 'Sandon, Kelshall'.

Link to Ride 5 Page 32

2 pages →

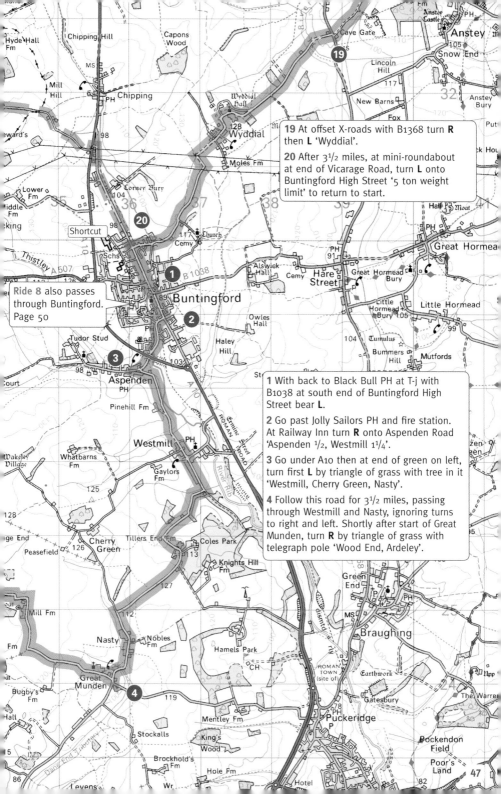

19 At offset X-roads with B1368 turn **R** then **L** 'Wyddial'.

20 After 3½ miles, at mini-roundabout at end of Vicarage Road, turn **L** onto Buntingford High Street '5 ton weight limit' to return to start.

Ride 8 also passes through Buntingford.
Page 50

1 With back to Black Bull PH at T-j with B1038 at south end of Buntingford High Street bear **L**.

2 Go past Jolly Sailors PH and fire station. At Railway Inn turn **R** onto Aspenden Road 'Aspenden ½, Westmill 1¼'.

3 Go under A10 then at end of green on left, turn first **L** by triangle of grass with tree in it 'Westmill, Cherry Green, Nasty'.

4 Follow this road for 3½ miles, passing through Westmill and Nasty, ignoring turns to right and left. Shortly after start of Great Munden, turn **R** by triangle of grass with telegraph pole 'Wood End, Ardeley'.

Shortcut

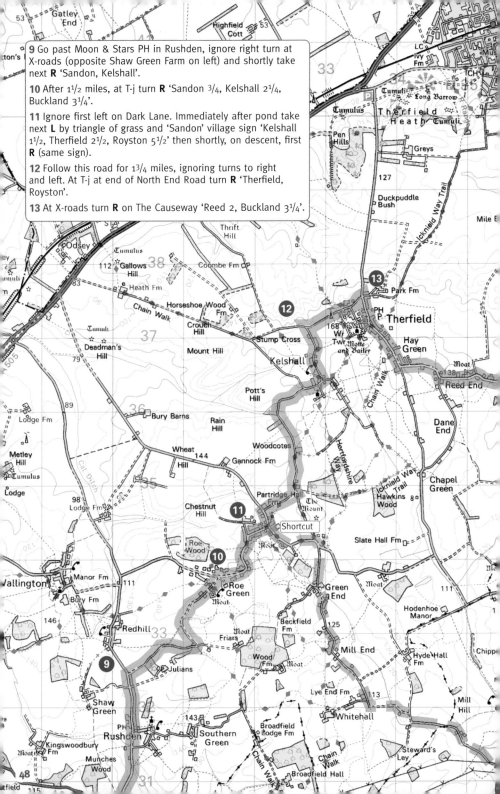

9 Go past Moon & Stars PH in Rushden, ignore right turn at X-roads (opposite Shaw Green Farm on left) and shortly take next **R** 'Sandon, Kelshall'.

10 After 1½ miles, at T-j turn **R** 'Sandon ¾, Kelshall 2¼, Buckland 3¼'.

11 Ignore first left on Dark Lane. Immediately after pond take next **L** by triangle of grass and 'Sandon' village sign 'Kelshall 1½, Therfield 2½, Royston 5½' then shortly, on descent, first **R** (same sign).

12 Follow this road for 1¾ miles, ignoring turns to right and left. At T-j at end of North End Road turn **R** 'Therfield, Royston'.

13 At X-roads turn **R** on The Causeway 'Reed 2, Buckland 3¼'.

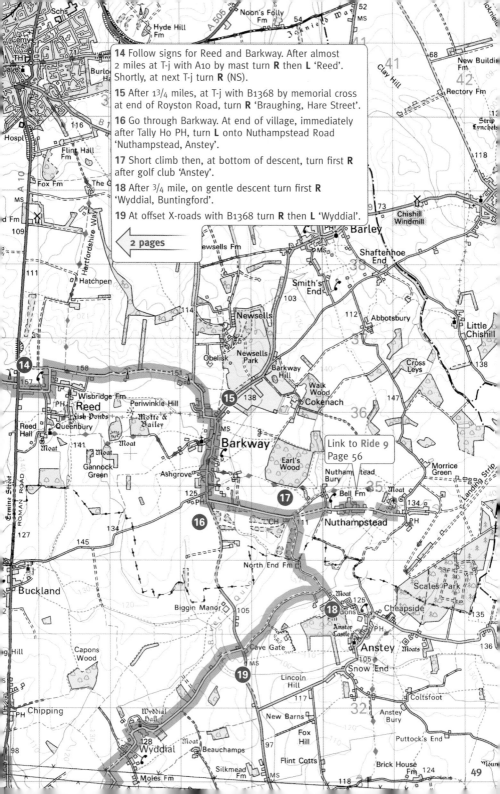

14 Follow signs for Reed and Barkway. After almost 2 miles at T-j with A10 by mast turn **R** then **L** 'Reed'. Shortly, at next T-j turn **R** (NS).

15 After 1³/₄ miles, at T-j with B1368 by memorial cross at end of Royston Road, turn **R** 'Braughing, Hare Street'.

16 Go through Barkway. At end of village, immediately after Tally Ho PH, turn **L** onto Nuthampstead Road 'Nuthampstead, Anstey'.

17 Short climb then, at bottom of descent, turn first **R** after golf club 'Anstey'.

18 After ³/₄ mile, on gentle descent turn first **R** 'Wyddial, Buntingford'.

19 At offset X-roads with B1368 turn **R** then **L** 'Wyddial'.

2 pages

Link to **Ride 9**
Page 56

West from Stansted Mountfitchet to Buntingford

Almost all of this easy route is on quiet lanes through the gently rolling arable land on the Essex / Hertfordshire border with several good pubs along the way. The ride starts from Stansted Mountfitchet with its motte-and-bailey castle, built in Norman times and now recreated, boasting a giant catapult, a thatched falconry and the white-washed Grand Hall. Down below is a row of well-preserved 16th-century houses. Other highlights on the ride include the crossing of the River Rib (a tributary of the River Lee) at Standon ford, the attractive village of Westmill with its tall-chimneyed houses, village green, tea room and pub, and the fine town of Buntingford, through which runs the old Roman Road of Ermine Street. On your way back to Stansted you will pass Manuden House, a Queen Anne mansion standing on a bend in The Street behind impressive iron railings, with gilded owls peering down from the gates.

NB This ride could easily be linked to Ride 7: leave Ride 8 (this ride) in Great Munden to join Ride 7 at Instruction 4 and follow through to Instruction 17, shortly after passing through Barkway. Follow signs for Anstey, rejoining Ride 8 at Instruction 20.

Overview

On-road ● 32 miles / 51 kilometres ● Easy

Start
The Tourist Information Centre /
Library, Crafton Green, Stansted
Mountfitchet

Parking
Car park at the back of the
library on Crafton Green

Busy roads
The roads through Stansted **1**
and Buntingford **17** to **18** all
have 30mph speed limits

Terrain
Undulating terrain between 200
and 400ft (60-120m) with no
major climbs

Nearest railway
Stansted Mountfitchet

Refreshments
Stansted Mountfitchet
Lots of choice

Hazel End
Three Horseshoes PH
T: 01279 813429

Hadham Ford
Nags Head PH
T: 01279 771555

Wellpond Green
Kick & Dicky PH
T: 01920 821424

Westmill
Sword in Hand PH
T: 01763 271356
Tearoom
T: 01763 274236

Buntingford
Lots of choice

Anstey
Blind Fiddler PH
T: 01763 848828

Brent Pelham
Black Horse PH
T: 01279 777305

Stocking Pelham
Brewery Tap
T: 01279 777280

Manuden
Yew Tree Inn
T: 01279 812888

Other rides nearby

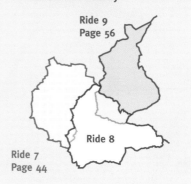

Ride 9
Page 56

Ride 8

Ride 7
Page 44

Map pages

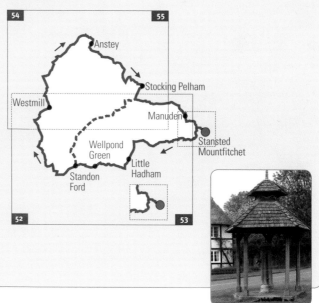

54 · 55 · Anstey · Stocking Pelham · Westmill · Manuden · Stansted Mountfitchet · Wellpond Green · Little Hadham · Standon Ford · 52 · 53

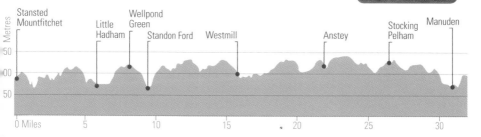

Metres · Stansted Mountfitchet · Little Hadham · Wellpond Green · Standon Ford · Westmill · Anstey · Stocking Pelham · Manuden · 50 · 00 · 50 · 0 Miles · 5 · 10 · 15 · 20 · 25 · 30

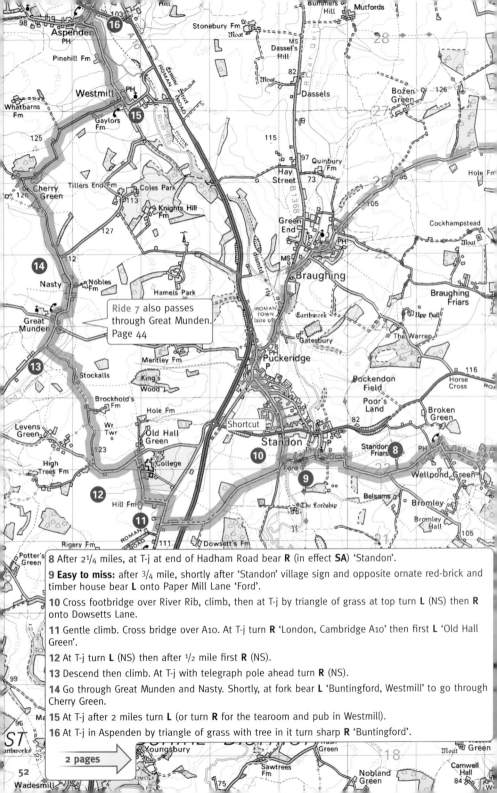

8 After 2¼ miles, at T-j at end of Hadham Road bear **R** (in effect **SA**) 'Standon'.

9 Easy to miss: after ¾ mile, shortly after 'Standon' village sign and opposite ornate red-brick and timber house bear **L** onto Paper Mill Lane 'Ford'.

10 Cross footbridge over River Rib, climb, then at T-j by triangle of grass at top turn **L** (NS) then **R** onto Dowsetts Lane.

11 Gentle climb. Cross bridge over A10. At T-j turn **R** 'London, Cambridge A10' then first **L** 'Old Hall Green'.

12 At T-j turn **L** (NS) then after ½ mile first **R** (NS).

13 Descend then climb. At T-j with telegraph pole ahead turn **R** (NS).

14 Go through Great Munden and Nasty. Shortly, at fork bear **L** 'Buntingford, Westmill' to go through Cherry Green.

15 At T-j after 2 miles turn **L** (or turn **R** for the tearoom and pub in Westmill).

16 At T-j in Aspenden by triangle of grass with tree in it turn sharp **R** 'Buntingford'.

Ride 7 also passes through Great Munden. Page 44

Shortcut

2 pages

52

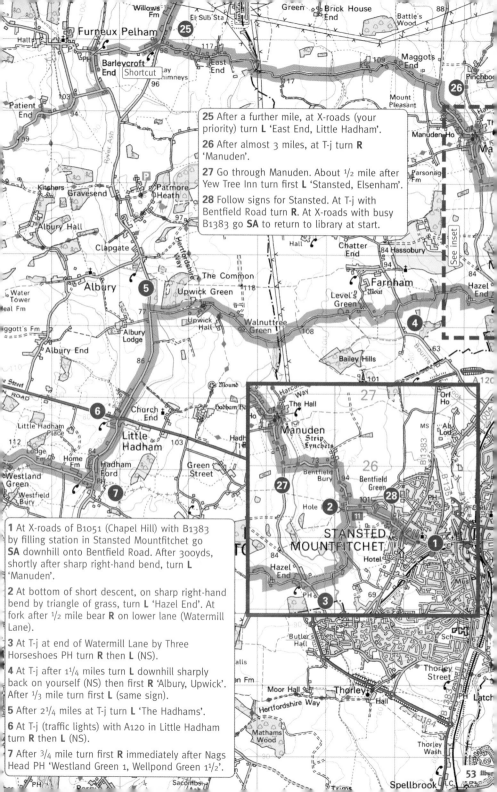

25 After a further mile, at X-roads (your priority) turn **L** 'East End, Little Hadham'.

26 After almost 3 miles, at T-j turn **R** 'Manuden'.

27 Go through Manuden. About ¹/₂ mile after Yew Tree Inn turn first **L** 'Stansted, Elsenham'.

28 Follow signs for Stansted. At T-j with Bentfield Road turn **R**. At X-roads with busy B1383 go **SA** to return to library at start.

1 At X-roads of B1051 (Chapel Hill) with B1383 by filling station in Stansted Mountfitchet go **SA** downhill onto Bentfield Road. After 300yds, shortly after sharp right-hand bend, turn **L** 'Manuden'.

2 At bottom of short descent, on sharp right-hand bend by triangle of grass, turn **L** 'Hazel End'. At fork after ¹/₂ mile bear **R** on lower lane (Watermill Lane).

3 At T-j at end of Watermill Lane by Three Horseshoes PH turn **R** then **L** (NS).

4 At T-j after 1¹/₄ miles turn **L** downhill sharply back on yourself (NS) then first **R** 'Albury, Upwick'. After ¹/₃ mile turn first **L** (same sign).

5 After 2¹/₄ miles at T-j turn **L** 'The Hadhams'.

6 At T-j (traffic lights) with A120 in Little Hadham turn **R** then **L** (NS).

7 After ³/₄ mile turn first **R** immediately after Nags Head PH 'Westland Green 1, Wellpond Green 1¹/₂'.

53 Albur

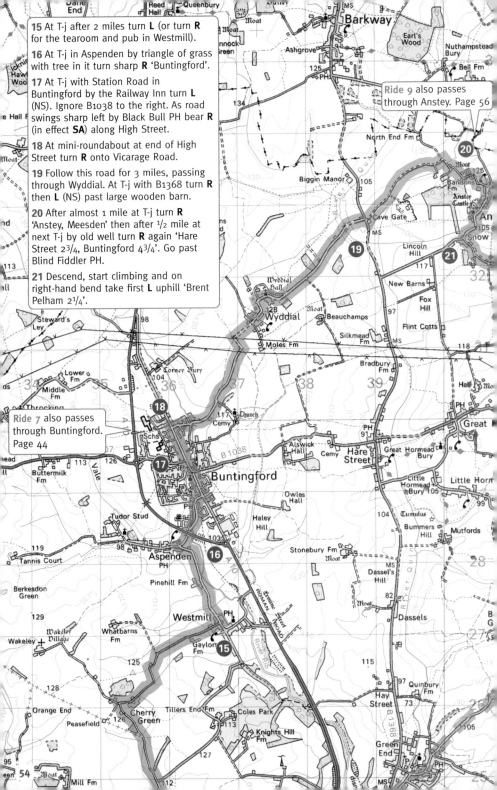

15 At T-j after 2 miles turn **L** (or turn **R** for the tearoom and pub in Westmill).

16 At T-j in Aspenden by triangle of grass with tree in it turn sharp **R** 'Buntingford'.

17 At T-j with Station Road in Buntingford by the Railway Inn turn **L** (NS). Ignore B1038 to the right. As road swings sharp left by Black Bull PH bear **R** (in effect **SA**) along High Street.

18 At mini-roundabout at end of High Street turn **R** onto Vicarage Road.

19 Follow this road for 3 miles, passing through Wyddial. At T-j with B1368 turn **R** then **L** (NS) past large wooden barn.

20 After almost 1 mile at T-j turn **R** 'Anstey, Meesden' then after ½ mile at next T-j by old well turn **R** again 'Hare Street 2¾, Buntingford 4¾'. Go past Blind Fiddler PH.

21 Descend, start climbing and on right-hand bend take first **L** uphill 'Brent Pelham 2¼'.

Ride 9 also passes through Anstey. Page 56

Ride 7 also passes through Buntingford. Page 44

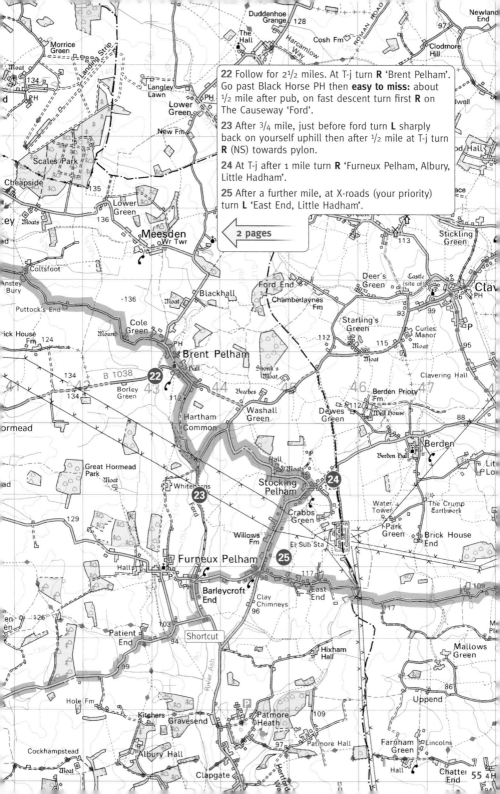

22 Follow for 2½ miles. At T-j turn **R** 'Brent Pelham'. Go past Black Horse PH then **easy to miss:** about ½ mile after pub, on fast descent turn first **R** on The Causeway 'Ford'.

23 After ¾ mile, just before ford turn **L** sharply back on yourself uphill then after ½ mile at T-j turn **R** (NS) towards pylon.

24 At T-j after 1 mile turn **R** 'Furneux Pelham, Albury, Little Hadham'.

25 After a further mile, at X-roads (your priority) turn **L** 'East End, Little Hadham'.

2 pages

Three Counties Ride south from Ickleton to the Pelhams

The ride starts from Ickleton, located just inside Cambridgeshire, but spends most of its course exploring the gently rolling arable landscape of north Hertfordshire and Essex. The

Roman Icknield Way passes close to Ickleton and it is probable that both names are taken from the ancient British Iceni tribe, led by Boudicca. A steady climb from Ickleton, located down

in the valley of the River Cam, leads southwest to Heydon and Great Chishill. Carefully avoiding the busier B roads, the route descends then climbs to the highpoint of the day at a dizzying 480ft (147m). Beyond Nuthampstead you follow an amazing wiggly open lane that feels as though it was built by a bunch of drunk navvies who couldn't walk straight. Furneux Pelham is the largest of the Pelham villages, named after the De Furneux family who owned all three villages in the 12th century. You may choose to sample a beer from the Brewery Tap. Onwards and northwards through Berden and the attractive village of Arkesden with its many thatched houses, tiny lanes lead on to Elmdon and the final climb of the day with huge views north towards the flat plain of Cambridgeshire.

Overview
On-road ● 34 miles / 54 kilometres ● Moderate

Start
Ickleton, northwest of
Saffron Walden

Parking
Village Hall car park in Ickleton,
opposite Church Street

Busy roads
Short section (less than ¼
mile) on B1039 just before
Elmdon **21**

Terrain
Undulating with one long
gentle climb at the start

Nearest railway
Great Chesterford

Refreshments
Ickleton
Ickleton Lion PH
T: 01799 530269

Heydon
King William IV PH
T: 01763 838773

Great Chishill
Pheasant PH
T: 01763 838535

Nuthampstead
Woodman PH
T: 01763 848328

Anstey
Blind Fiddler PH
T: 01763 848828

Great Hormead
Three Tuns PH
T: 01763 289409

Furneux Pelham
Brewery Tap PH
T: 01279 777280

Stocking Pelham
Cock PH
T: 01279 777217

Arkesden
Axe & Compasses PH
T: 01799 550272

Elmdon
Elmdon Dial PH
T: 01763 837386

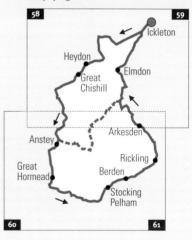

Other rides nearby

Ride 9

Ride 7
Page 44

Ride 8
Page 50

Map pages

58   59

Ickleton

Heydon

Elmdon

Great
Chishill

Anstey

Arkesden

Great
Hormead

Rickling

Berden

Stocking
Pelham

60   61

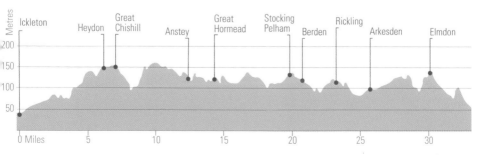

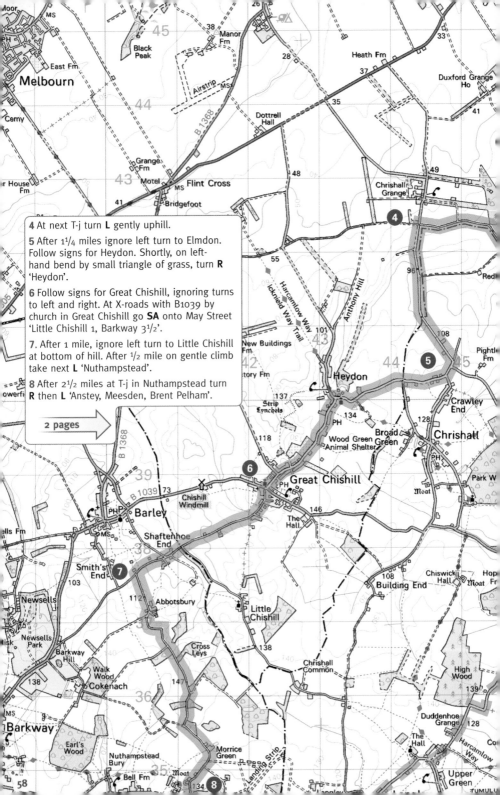

4 At next T-j turn **L** gently uphill.

5 After 1¼ miles ignore left turn to Elmdon. Follow signs for Heydon. Shortly, on left-hand bend by small triangle of grass, turn **R** 'Heydon'.

6 Follow signs for Great Chishill, ignoring turns to left and right. At X-roads with B1039 by church in Great Chishill go **SA** onto May Street 'Little Chishill 1, Barkway 3½'.

7. After 1 mile, ignore left turn to Little Chishill at bottom of hill. After ½ mile on gentle climb take next **L** 'Nuthampstead'.

8 After 2½ miles at T-j in Nuthampstead turn **R** then **L** 'Anstey, Meesden, Brent Pelham'.

2 pages ▶

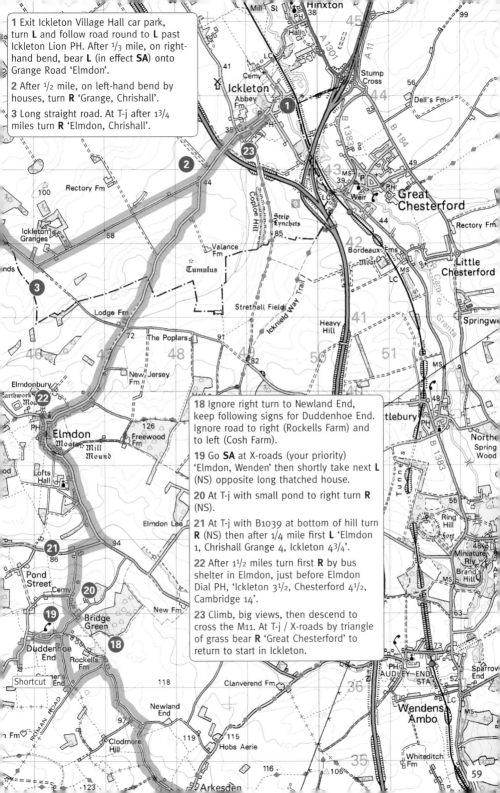

1 Exit Ickleton Village Hall car park, turn **L** and follow road round to **L** past Ickleton Lion PH. After 1/3 mile, on right-hand bend, bear **L** (in effect **SA**) onto Grange Road 'Elmdon'.

2 After 1/2 mile, on left-hand bend by houses, turn **R** 'Grange, Chrishall'.

3 Long straight road. At T-j after 13/4 miles turn **R** 'Elmdon, Chrishall'.

18 Ignore right turn to Newland End, keep following signs for Duddenhoe End. Ignore road to right (Rockells Farm) and to left (Cosh Farm).

19 Go **SA** at X-roads (your priority) 'Elmdon, Wenden' then shortly take next **L** (NS) opposite long thatched house.

20 At T-j with small pond to right turn **R** (NS).

21 At T-j with B1039 at bottom of hill turn **R** (NS) then after 1/4 mile first **L** 'Elmdon 1, Chrishall Grange 4, Ickleton 43/4'.

22 After 11/2 miles turn first **R** by bus shelter in Elmdon, just before Elmdon Dial PH, 'Ickleton 31/2, Chesterford 41/2, Cambridge 14'.

23 Climb, big views, then descend to cross the M11. At T-j / X-roads by triangle of grass bear **R** 'Great Chesterford' to return to start in Ickleton.

Link to **Ride 7**
Page 44

Ride 8 also passes
through Anstey. Page 50

8 After 2¹/₂ miles at T-j in Nuthampstead turn **R** then **L** 'Anstey, Meesden, Brent Pelham'.

9 At T-j in Anstey by triangle of grass with three trees in it, turn **R** 'Hare Street'. Go past Blind Fiddler PH.

10 After ¹/₂ mile ignore left to Brent Pelham. After further ¹/₃ mile take next **L** 'Flint Hall'.

11 Ignore left turn to Brick House Farm. At T-j with B1038 by Three Tuns PH turn **R** then **L** 'Little Hormead, Furneux Pelham'.

12 After ¹/₂ mile first **L** 'Little Hormead, Furneux Pelham'.

13 After 3 miles, at X-roads (your priority) by Brewery Tap PH in Furneux Pelham, go **SA** 'Stocking Pelham, Manuden' then after ¹/₂ mile at T-j turn **L** 'Stocking Pelham, Berden'.

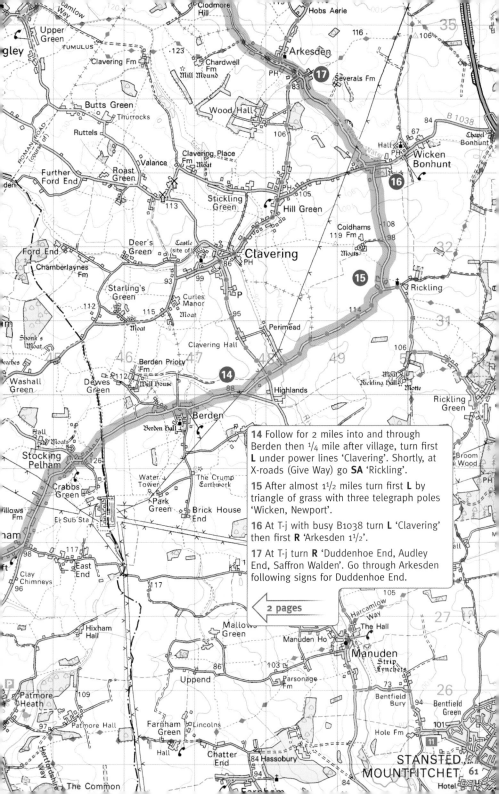

14 Follow for 2 miles into and through Berden then ¼ mile after village, turn first **L** under power lines 'Clavering'. Shortly, at X-roads (Give Way) go **SA** 'Rickling'.

15 After almost 1½ miles turn first **L** by triangle of grass with three telegraph poles 'Wicken, Newport'.

16 At T-j with busy B1038 turn **L** 'Clavering' then first **R** 'Arkesden 1½'.

17 At T-j turn **R** 'Duddenhoe End, Audley End, Saffron Walden'. Go through Arkesden following signs for Duddenhoe End.

← 2 pages

Thaxted, Finchingfield & Helions Bumpstead

The ride starts from the attractive village of Thaxted with its very fine Guildhall and myriad 15th- and 16th-century buildings decorated with elaborate plasterwork known as 'pargeting'. The elegant red-brick Clarence House, built in 1715, is where composer Gustav Holst worked on part of *The Planets*. Head east to Great Bardfield with its medieval and Georgian houses and a restored windmill. A little further north, Finchingfield is a jumble of medieval cottages and Georgian houses around the village green. This is an area with a dense network of lanes with options to amend, shorten or lengthen the rides: the aim is to avoid spending time on busy roads and to cross them directly from one quiet lane straight across to the next. All around lies rich arable land with occasional stands of broadleaf woodland the terrain is undulating, almost all the land lying between 200-400ft (60-120m) The pubs appear at regular intervals along the way, at Helions Bumpstead, Ashdon, Howlett End and Debden. At times it appears that the villages are trying to outdo each other with the splendou of their village signs, often located on the village green.

Overview

On-road ● 34 miles / 54 kilometres ● Easy / Moderate

Start
Thaxted, northeast of Bishop's Stortford

Parking
Free car park on Margaret Street, near the church

Busy roads
Short section on B184 between Wimbish and Debden **14**

Terrain
Gently undulating, no steep climbs

Nearest railway
Newport

Refreshments
Thaxted
Lots of choice

Great Bardfield
Bell Inn
T: 01373 811097
Vine PH
T: 01371 810355

Finchingfield
Lots of choice

Helions Bumpstead
Three Horseshoes PH
T: 01440 730298

Ashdon
Rose and Crown PH
T: 01799 584337

Howlett End (Wimbish)
White Hart PH
01799 599030

Debden
Plough PH
T: 01799 541899

Map pages

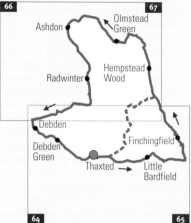

Other rides nearby

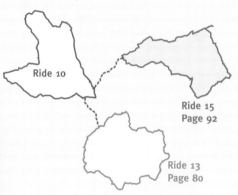

Ride 10

Ride 15
Page 92

Ride 13
Page 80

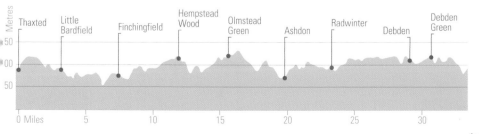

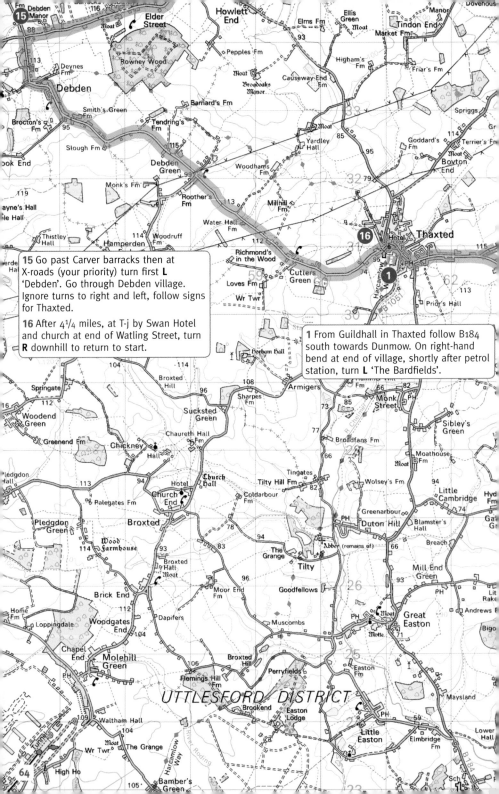

15 Go past Carver barracks then at X-roads (your priority) turn first **L** 'Debden'. Go through Debden village. Ignore turns to right and left, follow signs for Thaxted.

16 After 4¼ miles, at T-j by Swan Hotel and church at end of Watling Street, turn **R** downhill to return to start.

1 From Guildhall in Thaxted follow B184 south towards Dunmow. On right-hand bend at end of village, shortly after petrol station, turn **L** 'The Bardfields'.

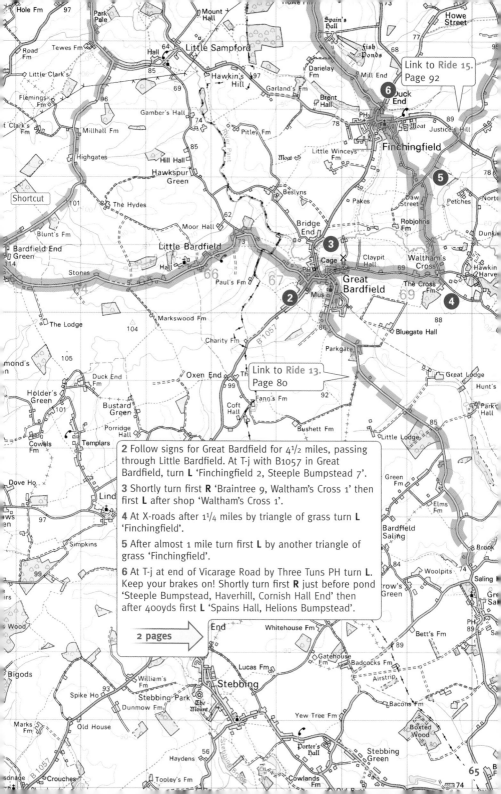

Link to **Ride 15**. Page 92

Link to **Ride 13**. Page 80

2 Follow signs for Great Bardfield for 4¹/₂ miles, passing through Little Bardfield. At T-j with B1057 in Great Bardfield, turn **L** 'Finchingfield 2, Steeple Bumpstead 7'.

3 Shortly turn first **R** 'Braintree 9, Waltham's Cross 1' then first **L** after shop 'Waltham's Cross 1'.

4 At X-roads after 1¹/₄ miles by triangle of grass turn **L** 'Finchingfield'.

5 After almost 1 mile turn first **L** by another triangle of grass 'Finchingfield'.

6 At T-j at end of Vicarage Road by Three Tuns PH turn **L**. Keep your brakes on! Shortly turn first **R** just before pond 'Steeple Bumpstead, Haverhill, Cornish Hall End' then after 400yds first **L** 'Spains Hall, Helions Bumpstead'.

2 pages ➡

65

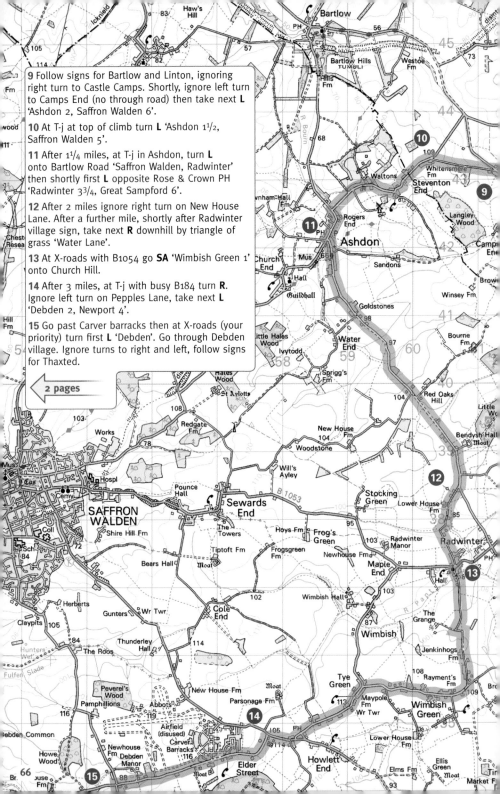

9 Follow signs for Bartlow and Linton, ignoring right turn to Castle Camps. Shortly, ignore left turn to Camps End (no through road) then take next **L** 'Ashdon 2, Saffron Walden 6'.

10 At T-j at top of climb turn **L** 'Ashdon 1½, Saffron Walden 5'.

11 After 1¼ miles, at T-j in Ashdon, turn **L** onto Bartlow Road 'Saffron Walden, Radwinter' then shortly first **L** opposite Rose & Crown PH 'Radwinter 3¾, Great Sampford 6'.

12 After 2 miles ignore right turn on New House Lane. After a further mile, shortly after Radwinter village sign, take next **R** downhill by triangle of grass 'Water Lane'.

13 At X-roads with B1054 go **SA** 'Wimbish Green 1' onto Church Hill.

14 After 3 miles, at T-j with busy B184 turn **R**. Ignore left turn on Pepples Lane, take next **L** 'Debden 2, Newport 4'.

15 Go past Carver barracks then at X-roads (your priority) turn first **L** 'Debden'. Go through Debden village. Ignore turns to right and left, follow signs for Thaxted.

← 2 pages

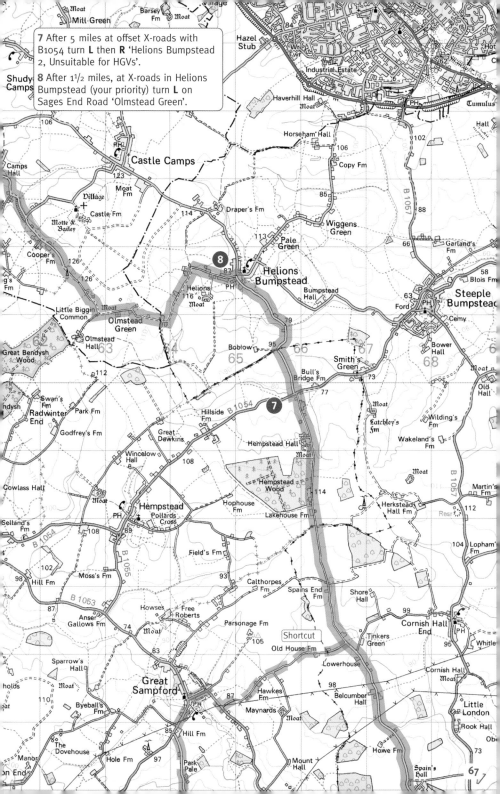

7 After 5 miles at offset X-roads with B1054 turn **L** then **R** 'Helions Bumpstead 2, Unsuitable for HGVs'.

8 After 1½ miles, at X-roads in Helions Bumpstead (your priority) turn **L** on Sages End Road 'Olmstead Green'.

Takeley, Good Easter & Pleshey

Located equidistant from Harlow, Chelmsford, Bishop's Stortford and Braintree, this ride nevertheless links together mile after mile of delightfully quiet lanes through the area known as The Rodings: there are no fewer than eight villages and hamlets in the Rodings clan (Abbess, Aythorpe, Beauchamp, Berners, High, Leaden, Margaret and White). The ride heads south from Takeley, located just a mile or so south of Stansted airport so be prepared for planes at the start and finish. After passing through or near several of the Rodings, you

turn northeast and head for the village of Pleshey. Little is now left of Pleshey's once mighty castle, built by Geoffrey de Mandeville soon after the Norman Conquest. It was so important that it was home to successive Lord High Constables of England for more than 200 years. The only building that survives is the 15th-century bridge of red brick that connects the mound with the inner bailey. The fall of Pleshey Castle is even mentioned in Shakespeare:

'Alack, and what shall good old York here see,
But empty lodgings and unfurnished walls,
Unpeopled offices, untrodden stones...'

Running east and west from Takeley is the recreational railway path known as the Flitch Way. The western section of the trail lies near Takeley. A better quality stretch lies further east, connecting Little Dunmow to Braintree.

Overview
On-road ● 24 miles / 38 kilometres ● Easy / Moderate

Start
Takeley, 4 miles east of
Bishop's Stortford

Parking
On Roding Drive, a new
development on the east side
of Takeley, along the B1256
towards Great Dunmow. Roding
Drive is on the north side of
the B1256, about ½ mile east
of the crossroads / traffic lights
in the centre of the village

Busy roads
The B1256 (was the old A120)
in Takeley is busy. It is crossed
almost directly ❶

Terrain
Undulating with no
significant climbs

Nearest railway
Sawbridgeworth

Refreshments
Takeley
Lots of choice

White Roding
Black Horse PH
T: 01279 876322

Fyfield
Black Bull PH
T: 01277 899225
Queens Head PH
T: 01277 899231

Great Waltham
Beehive PH
T: 01245 360356

Pleshey
Leather Bottle PH
T: 01245 237291
White Horse PH
T: 01245 237281

Other rides nearby

Ride 11

Ride 12
Page 74

Map pages

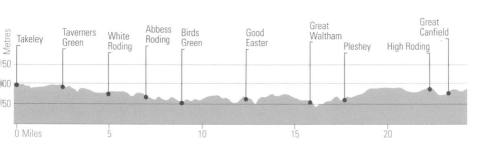

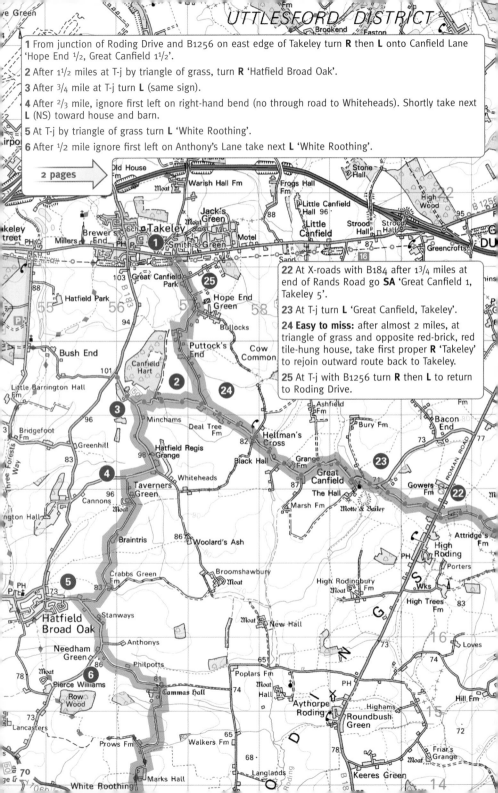

1 From junction of Roding Drive and B1256 on east edge of Takeley turn **R** then **L** onto Canfield Lane 'Hope End ½, Great Canfield 1½'.

2 After 1½ miles at T-j by triangle of grass, turn **R** 'Hatfield Broad Oak'.

3 After ¾ mile at T-j turn **L** (same sign).

4 After ⅔ mile, ignore first left on right-hand bend (no through road to Whiteheads). Shortly take next **L** (NS) toward house and barn.

5 At T-j by triangle of grass turn **L** 'White Roothing'.

6 After ½ mile ignore first left on Anthony's Lane take next **L** 'White Roothing'.

2 pages

22 At X-roads with B184 after 1¾ miles at end of Rands Road go **SA** 'Great Canfield 1, Takeley 5'.

23 At T-j turn **L** 'Great Canfield, Takeley'.

24 Easy to miss: after almost 2 miles, at triangle of grass and opposite red-brick, red tile-hung house, take first proper **R** 'Takeley' to rejoin outward route back to Takeley.

25 At T-j with B1256 turn **R** then **L** to return to Roding Drive.

17 Just after start of houses in Pleshey turn **R** on Back Lane (just before Leather Bottle PH) and shortly **R** again on Vicarage Road 'Pleshey Grange'.

18 Follow signs Pleshey Grange, ignoring turns to right and left. After 1½ miles, at T-j by large triangle of grass turn **R** 'Dunmow, Barnston, Felsted'.

19 After ½ mile at T-j turn **L** 'High Roding'.

20 Ignore turns to Stagden Cross and Pleshey, follow signs for Roothings and Dunmow. At T-j turn **L** 'High Easter' then **R** 'The Rodings'.

21 After ½ mile first **R** 'High Roding, Great Canfield'.

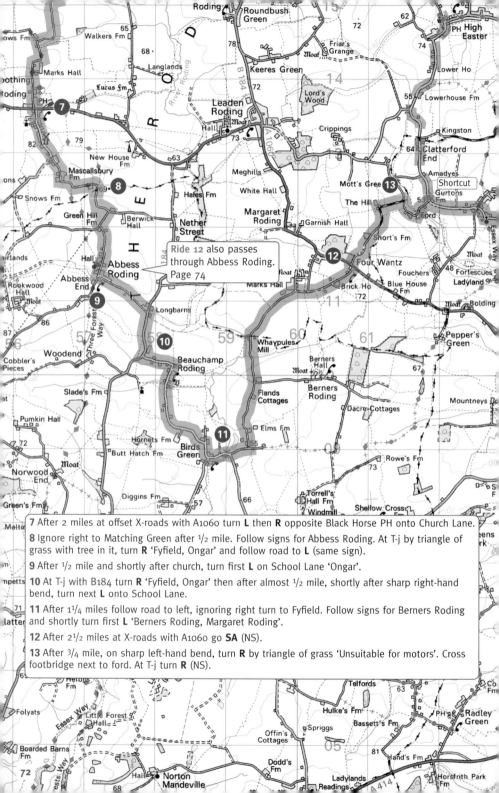

Ride 12 also passes through Abbess Roding. Page 74

7 After 2 miles at offset X-roads with A1060 turn **L** then **R** opposite Black Horse PH onto Church Lane.

8 Ignore right to Matching Green after ½ mile. Follow signs for Abbess Roding. At T-j by triangle of grass with tree in it, turn **R** 'Fyfield, Ongar' and follow road to **L** (same sign).

9 After ½ mile and shortly after church, turn first **L** on School Lane 'Ongar'.

10 At T-j with B184 turn **R** 'Fyfield, Ongar' then after almost ½ mile, shortly after sharp right-hand bend, turn next **L** onto School Lane.

11 After 1¼ miles follow road to left, ignoring right turn to Fyfield. Follow signs for Berners Roding and shortly turn first **L** 'Berners Roding, Margaret Roding'.

12 After 2½ miles at X-roads with A1060 go **SA** (NS).

13 After ¾ mile, on sharp left-hand bend, turn **R** by triangle of grass 'Unsuitable for motors'. Cross footbridge next to ford. At T-j turn **R** (NS).

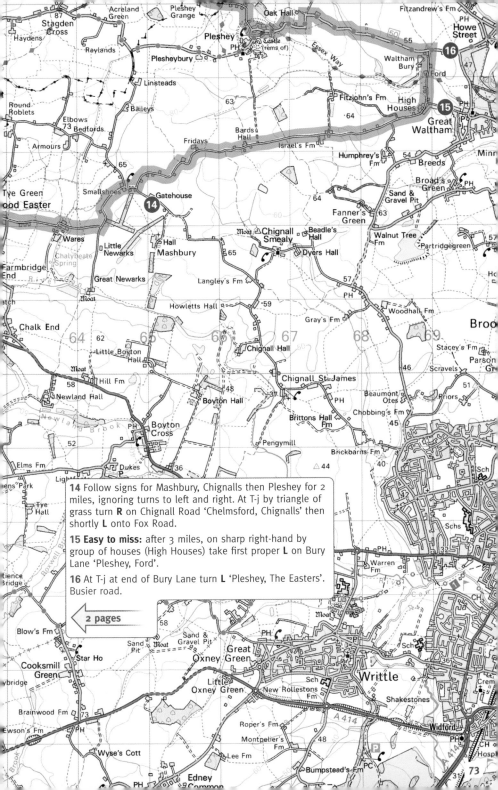

14 Follow signs for Mashbury, Chignalls then Pleshey for 2 miles, ignoring turns to left and right. At T-j by triangle of grass turn **R** on Chignall Road 'Chelmsford, Chignalls' then shortly **L** onto Fox Road.

15 Easy to miss: after 3 miles, on sharp right-hand by group of houses (High Houses) take first proper **L** on Bury Lane 'Pleshey, Ford'.

16 At T-j at end of Bury Lane turn **L** 'Pleshey, The Easters'. Busier road.

2 pages

West from Writtle to The Rodings

All around Writtle's green are houses of different styles, from the Tudor-timbered splendour of Aubyns, near the church, through elegant Georgian brickwork to varieties of pargeted plaster. Writtle's other claim to fame is that in 1899, Marconi, the inventor of radio, began making transmissions from here, raising his aerials on the flat land by the River Wid. A traffic-free section of the National Cycle Network links Writtle to Chelmsford providing a safe route to the start of the network of quiet lanes that lead westwards to the Rodings. For a ride that picks and weaves its way among the region's bewildering network of quiet lanes, it comes as a pleasant surprise that you follow the same one for seven miles without turning off to right or left from the outskirts of Chelmsford all the way to High Easter, where there is a fine pub. The ride continues southwards through rich agricultural country to Fyfield, beyond which it becomes slightly more fractured as it twists and turns its way back to the start.

Overview

On-road ● 28 miles / 45 kilometres ● Easy

Start
The Inn on the Green, Writtle,
west of Chelmsford

Parking
Car park off the green

Busy roads
3/4 mile on the A1060 to the
east of White Roding 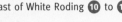 to

Terrain
Gently undulating with
no major climbs

Nearest railway
Chelmsford 1 mile east
of the route at the start

Refreshments
Writtle
Lots of choice

Chignall St James
Three Elms PH
T: 01245 440496

North of Mashbury
Fox Inn
T: 01245 231573

High Easter
Cock & Bell Inn
T: 01245 231296
Punchbowl PH
T: 01245 231222

Pleshey, just off the route
Leather Bottle PH
T: 01245 237291
White Horse PH
T: 01245 237281

Aythorpe Roding
Axe & Compasses PH
T: 01279 876648

White Roding
Black Horse PH
T: 01279 876322

Fyfield
Black Bull PH
T: 01277 899225
Queens Head PH
T: 01277 899231

Radley Green
Cuckoo Inn
T: 01245 248946

Newney Green
Duck Inn
T: 01245 421894

Other rides nearby

Ride 11
Page 68

Ride 12

Map pages

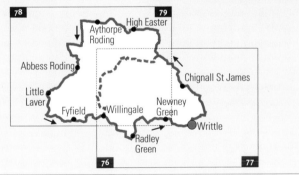

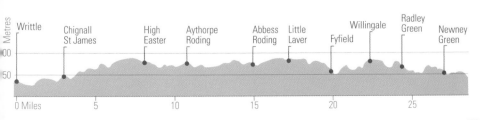

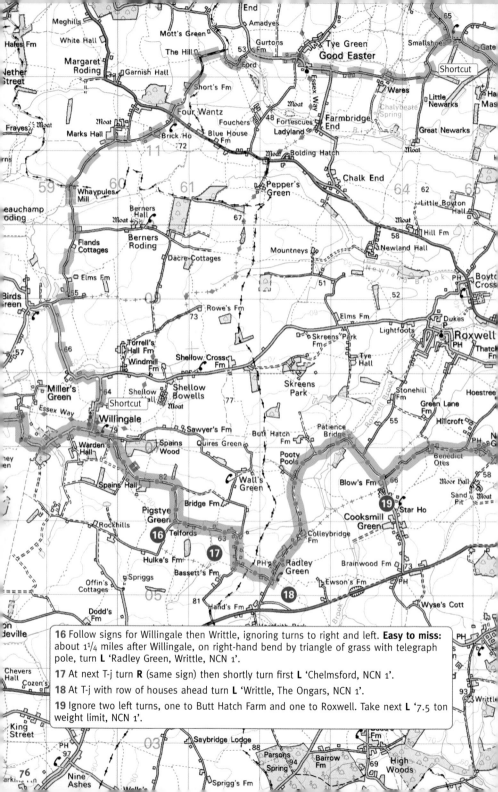

16 Follow signs for Willingale then Writtle, ignoring turns to right and left. **Easy to miss:** about 1¼ miles after Willingale, on right-hand bend by triangle of grass with telegraph pole, turn **L** 'Radley Green, Writtle, NCN 1'.

17 At next T-j turn **R** (same sign) then shortly turn first **L** 'Chelmsford, NCN 1'.

18 At T-j with row of houses ahead turn **L** 'Writtle, The Ongars, NCN 1'.

19 Ignore two left turns, one to Butt Hatch Farm and one to Roxwell. Take next **L** '7.5 ton weight limit, NCN 1'.

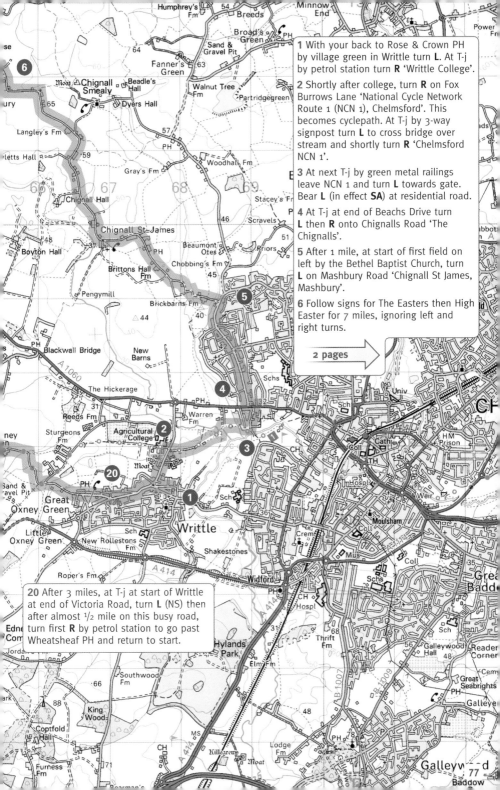

1 With your back to Rose & Crown PH by village green in Writtle turn **L**. At T-j by petrol station turn **R** 'Writtle College'.

2 Shortly after college, turn **R** on Fox Burrows Lane 'National Cycle Network Route 1 (NCN 1), Chelmsford'. This becomes cyclepath. At T-j by 3-way signpost turn **L** to cross bridge over stream and shortly turn **R** 'Chelmsford NCN 1'.

3 At next T-j by green metal railings leave NCN 1 and turn **L** towards gate. Bear **L** (in effect **SA**) at residential road.

4 At T-j at end of Beachs Drive turn **L** then **R** onto Chignalls Road 'The Chignalls'.

5 After 1 mile, at start of first field on left by the Bethel Baptist Church, turn **L** on Mashbury Road 'Chignall St James, Mashbury'.

6 Follow signs for The Easters then High Easter for 7 miles, ignoring left and right turns.

2 pages →

20 After 3 miles, at T-j at start of Writtle at end of Victoria Road, turn **L** (NS) then after almost ½ mile on this busy road, turn first **R** by petrol station to go past Wheatsheaf PH and return to start.

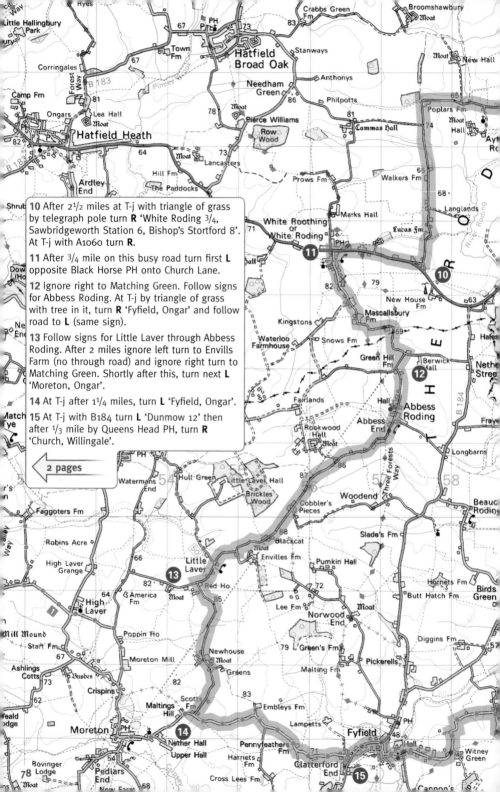

10 After 2½ miles at T-j with triangle of grass by telegraph pole turn **R** 'White Roding ¾, Sawbridgeworth Station 6, Bishop's Stortford 8'. At T-j with A1060 turn **R**.

11 After ¾ mile on this busy road turn first **L** opposite Black Horse PH onto Church Lane.

12 Ignore right to Matching Green. Follow signs for Abbess Roding. At T-j by triangle of grass with tree in it, turn **R** 'Fyfield, Ongar' and follow road to **L** (same sign).

13 Follow signs for Little Laver through Abbess Roding. After 2 miles ignore left turn to Envills Farm (no through road) and ignore right turn to Matching Green. Shortly after this, turn next **L** 'Moreton, Ongar'.

14 At T-j after 1¼ miles, turn **L** 'Fyfield, Ongar'.

15 At T-j with B184 turn **L** 'Dunmow 12' then after ⅓ mile by Queens Head PH, turn **R** 'Church, Willingale'.

2 pages

7 About ¼ mile after Punchbowl PH and church in High Easter, on sharp left-hand bend shortly after last of houses, bear **R** (NS).

8 After ¾ mile at T-j by triangle of grass on bend bear **L** 'Aythorpe Roding'.

9 Ignore left turn to Keeres Green. At X-roads with B184 by Axe & Compasses PH go **SA** 'Aythorpe Roding Church'.

Ride **11** also passes through Smallshoes. Page 68

Ring around Braintree from Great Leighs

Rides that form a ring about 5-10 miles around somewhere like Braintree tend to avoid busy roads as you are crossing the 'spokes' that lead to the hub or centre of town. In the case of Braintree, as a bonus, one of these 'spokes' is the traffic-free railway path known as the Flitch Way which starts at the back of Braintree railway station, so the ride could just as easily be started from the centre of Braintree and joined just to the north of Felsted. As described here, the ride starts from Great Leighs. Soon after crossing two of the busier roads radiating out from Braintree (the B1018 and A120) you come to the village of Stisted, with a café much beloved by cyclists and some of the most extraordinarily tall and ornate chimneys you are ever likely to come across. Skirting close to the northern edge of Braintree, the ride heads northwest to cross the River Pant near Church End. You may wish to divert off the route to visit Stebbing, whose buildings date from the Middle Ages - many of these are decorated with pargeting on their façades. There is also an 18th-century water mill. The Great Mount earthwork is the site of the castle built by Ranulf Peverel soon after the Norman Conquest.

Overview

On-road ● 30 miles / 48 kilometres ● Easy / Moderate

Start
Great Leighs Village Hall,
off the A131 about 4 miles
southwest of Braintree

Parking
As above

Busy roads
● Take care crossing the busy
A120 south of Stisted and
the A131 north of Braintree ⑯

● Busier section through
Bocking (30mph speed limit)
⑰

Terrain
Undulating

Nearest railway
Braintree

Refreshments
Great Leighs
Lots of choice

White Notley
Cross Keys PH
T: 01376 583297

Cressing
The Willows
T: 01376 583399

Stisted
Specialities Tearooms
T: 01376 339228
Onley Arms PH
T: 01376 325204

Bocking Churchstreet
Rose & Crown PH
T: 01376 324661

Church End
Teas at village store.

Felsted
Swan PH
T: 01371 820245
Chequers PH
T: 01371 820226

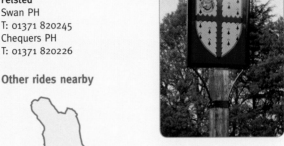

Other rides nearby

Ride 10
Page 62

Ride 13

Ride 14
Page 86

Map pages

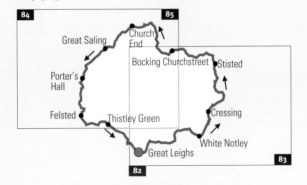

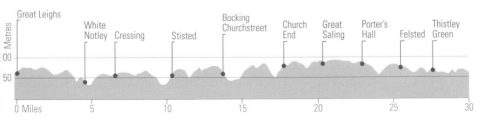

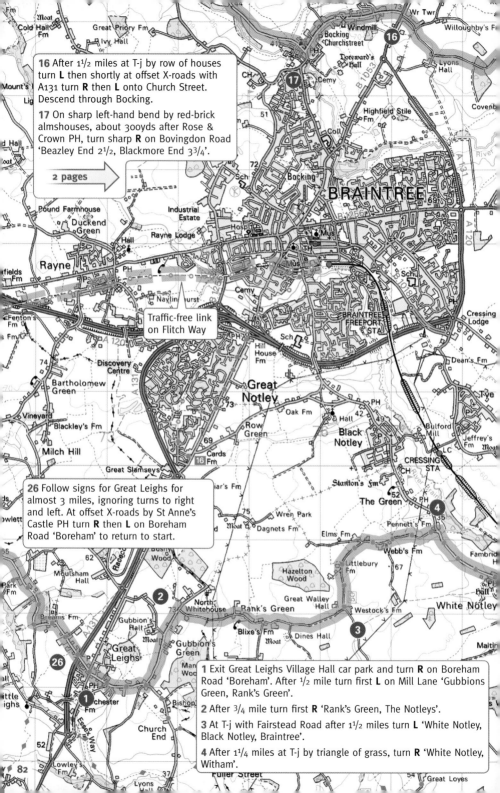

16 After 1½ miles at T-j by row of houses turn **L** then shortly at offset X-roads with A131 turn **R** then **L** onto Church Street. Descend through Bocking.

17 On sharp left-hand bend by red-brick almshouses, about 300yds after Rose & Crown PH, turn sharp **R** on Bovingdon Road 'Beazley End 2½, Blackmore End 3¾'.

2 pages ➡

Traffic-free link on Flitch Way

26 Follow signs for Great Leighs for almost 3 miles, ignoring turns to right and left. At offset X-roads by St Anne's Castle PH turn **R** then **L** on Boreham Road 'Boreham' to return to start.

1 Exit Great Leighs Village Hall car park and turn **R** on Boreham Road 'Boreham'. After ½ mile turn first **L** on Mill Lane 'Gubbions Green, Rank's Green'.

2 After ¾ mile turn first **R** 'Rank's Green, The Notleys'.

3 At T-j with Fairstead Road after 1½ miles turn **L** 'White Notley, Black Notley, Braintree'.

4 After 1¼ miles at T-j by triangle of grass, turn **R** 'White Notley, Witham'.

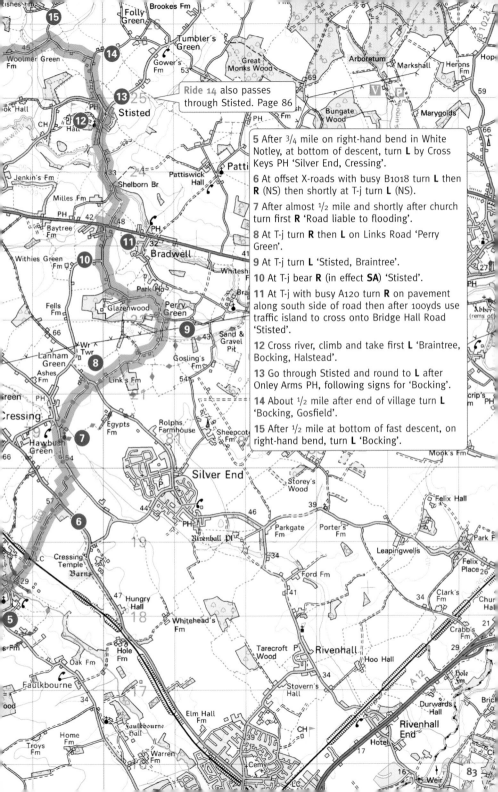

Ride 14 also passes through Stisted. Page 86

5 After ¾ mile on right-hand bend in White Notley, at bottom of descent, turn **L** by Cross Keys PH 'Silver End, Cressing'.

6 At offset X-roads with busy B1018 turn **L** then **R** (NS) then shortly at T-j turn **L** (NS).

7 After almost ½ mile and shortly after church turn first **R** 'Road liable to flooding'.

8 At T-j turn **R** then **L** on Links Road 'Perry Green'.

9 At T-j turn **L** 'Stisted, Braintree'.

10 At T-j bear **R** (in effect **SA**) 'Stisted'.

11 At T-j with busy A120 turn **R** on pavement along south side of road then after 100yds use traffic island to cross onto Bridge Hall Road 'Stisted'.

12 Cross river, climb and take first **L** 'Braintree, Bocking, Halstead'.

13 Go through Stisted and round to **L** after Onley Arms PH, following signs for 'Bocking'.

14 About ½ mile after end of village turn **L** 'Bocking, Gosfield'.

15 After ½ mile at bottom of fast descent, on right-hand bend, turn **L** 'Bocking'.

83

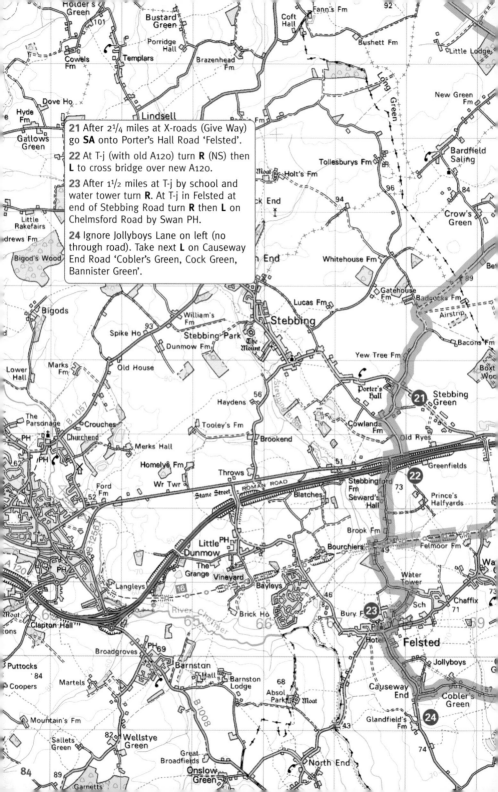

21 After 2¼ miles at X-roads (Give Way) go **SA** onto Porter's Hall Road 'Felsted'.

22 At T-j (with old A120) turn **R** (NS) then **L** to cross bridge over new A120.

23 After 1½ miles at T-j by school and water tower turn **R**. At T-j in Felsted at end of Stebbing Road turn **R** then **L** on Chelmsford Road by Swan PH.

24 Ignore Jollyboys Lane on left (no through road). Take next **L** on Causeway End Road 'Cobler's Green, Cock Green, Bannister Green'.

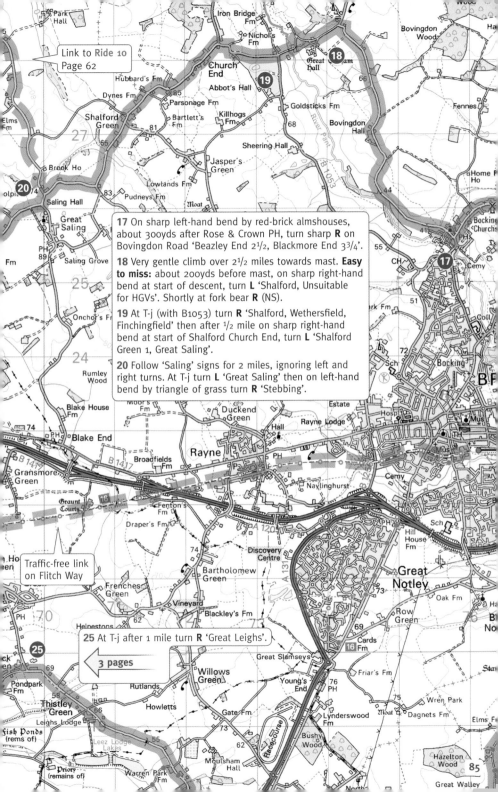

Link to **Ride 10** Page 62

17 On sharp left-hand bend by red-brick almshouses, about 300yds after Rose & Crown PH, turn sharp **R** on Bovingdon Road 'Beazley End 2½, Blackmore End 3¾'.

18 Very gentle climb over 2½ miles towards mast. **Easy to miss:** about 200yds before mast, on sharp right-hand bend at start of descent, turn **L** 'Shalford, Unsuitable for HGVs'. Shortly at fork bear **R** (NS).

19 At T-j (with B1053) turn **R** 'Shalford, Wethersfield, Finchingfield' then after ½ mile on sharp right-hand bend at start of Shalford Church End, turn **L** 'Shalford Green 1, Great Saling'.

20 Follow 'Saling' signs for 2 miles, ignoring left and right turns. At T-j turn **L** 'Great Saling' then on left-hand bend by triangle of grass turn **R** 'Stebbing'.

Traffic-free link on Flitch Way

25 At T-j after 1 mile turn **R** 'Great Leighs'.

3 pages

85

Ride 14

Coggeshall & the Colne Valley

Coggeshall grew rich in the Middle Ages from the wool and cloth trade and is noted for its merchants' houses with their intricate woodcarving. The finest example is Paycocke's House, dating from 1500. Coggeshall Abbey was founded in 1140 and taken over by Cistercian monks, who learnt the art of brick-making from sister houses on the continent and thus re-established brick manufacture in England for the first time since the departure of the Romans. The ride heads east on quiet lanes through Great Tey and Fordham before turning west, passing close by the East Anglian Railway Museum at Chappel and Wakes Colne Station, complete with steam trains. A network of tiny lanes crosses the gently rolling countryside past copses of broadleaf woodland to Pebmarsh. Turn south to re-cross the Colne Valley at Bunting's Green, heading for the delights of Stisted, with its pub, tearoom popular with cyclists and a fine display of massive ornamental chimneys on many of the buildings. The A120 is crossed to the south of Stisted, giving you the quietest option for returning back to Coggeshall along the valley of the River Blackwater.

Overview
On-road ● **32 miles / 51 kilometres** ● **Easy**

Start
The clocktower in Coggeshall, west of Colchester

Parking
Car park by the Library on Stoneham Street (off the street north of the clocktower)

Busy roads
● Take great care crossing the A120 on the east side of Coggeshall **3**

● A short section of the A1124 is used through Fordstreet **9**

● The second crossing of the A120 near Stisted is easier as there is a traffic island **25**

Terrain
Undulating with no major hills

Nearest railway
Kelvedon

Refreshments
Coggeshall
Lots of choice

Great Tey
Chequers PH
T: 01206 210814

Fordstreet
Coopers Arms PH
T: 01206 241177
Old Queens Head PH
T: 01206 241584
Shoulder of Mutton PH
T: 01206 240464

Stisted
Specialities Tearooms
T: 01376 339228
Onley Arms PH
T: 01376 325204

Other rides nearby

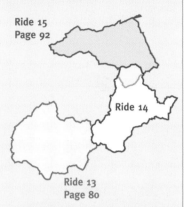

Ride 15
Page 92

Ride 14

Ride 13
Page 80

Map pages

90   91
Pebmarsh
Daws Cross
Chappel
Burton's Green
Fordham
Stisted
Great Aldham Tey
Coggeshall
Perry Green
88   89

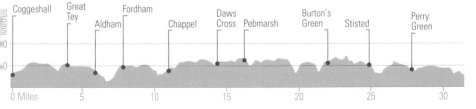

Coggeshall   Great Tey   Aldham   Fordham   Chappel   Daws Cross   Pebmarsh   Burton's Green   Stisted   Perry Green

0 Miles   5   10   15   20   25   30

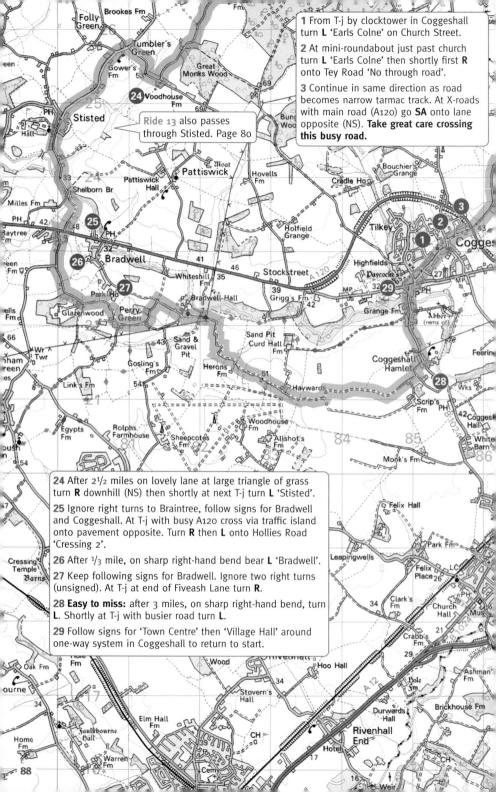

1 From T-j by clocktower in Coggeshall turn **L** 'Earls Colne' on Church Street.

2 At mini-roundabout just past church turn **L** 'Earls Colne' then shortly first **R** onto Tey Road 'No through road'.

3 Continue in same direction as road becomes narrow tarmac track. At X-roads with main road (A120) go **SA** onto lane opposite (NS). **Take great care crossing this busy road.**

Ride 13 also passes through Stisted. Page 80

24 After 2½ miles on lovely lane at large triangle of grass turn **R** downhill (NS) then shortly at next T-j turn **L** 'Stisted'.

25 Ignore right turns to Braintree, follow signs for Bradwell and Coggeshall. At T-j with busy A120 cross via traffic island onto pavement opposite. Turn **R** then **L** onto Hollies Road 'Cressing 2'.

26 After ⅓ mile, on sharp right-hand bend bear **L** 'Bradwell'.

27 Keep following signs for Bradwell. Ignore two right turns (unsigned). At T-j at end of Fiveash Lane turn **R**.

28 **Easy to miss:** after 3 miles, on sharp right-hand bend, turn **L**. Shortly at T-j with busier road turn **L**.

29 Follow signs for 'Town Centre' then 'Village Hall' around one-way system in Coggeshall to return to start.

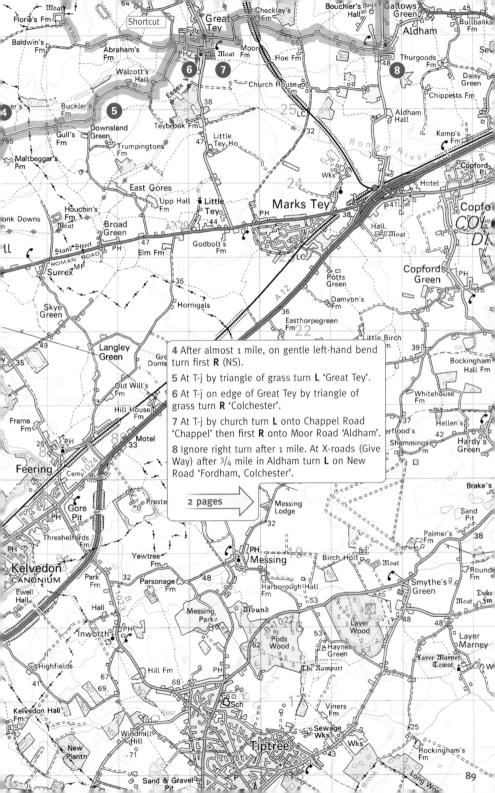

4 After almost 1 mile, on gentle left-hand bend turn first **R** (NS).

5 At T-j by triangle of grass turn **L** 'Great Tey'.

6 At T-j on edge of Great Tey by triangle of grass turn **R** 'Colchester'.

7 At T-j by church turn **L** onto Chappel Road 'Chappel' then first **R** onto Moor Road 'Aldham'.

8 Ignore right turn after 1 mile. At X-roads (Give Way) after 3/4 mile in Aldham turn **L** on New Road 'Fordham, Colchester'.

2 pages →

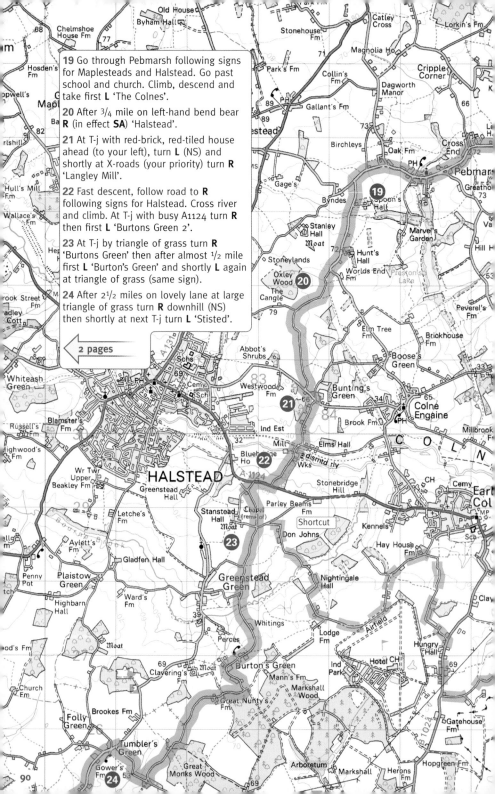

19 Go through Pebmarsh following signs for Maplesteads and Halstead. Go past school and church. Climb, descend and take first **L** 'The Colnes'.

20 After 3/4 mile on left-hand bend bear **R** (in effect **SA**) 'Halstead'.

21 At T-j with red-brick, red-tiled house ahead (to your left), turn **L** (NS) and shortly at X-roads (your priority) turn **R** 'Langley Mill'.

22 Fast descent, follow road to **R** following signs for Halstead. Cross river and climb. At T-j with busy A1124 turn **R** then first **L** 'Burtons Green 2'.

23 At T-j by triangle of grass turn **R** 'Burtons Green' then after almost 1/2 mile first **L** 'Burton's Green' and shortly **L** again at triangle of grass (same sign).

24 After 2 1/2 miles on lovely lane at large triangle of grass turn **R** downhill (NS) then shortly at next T-j turn **L** 'Stisted'.

◁ **2 pages**

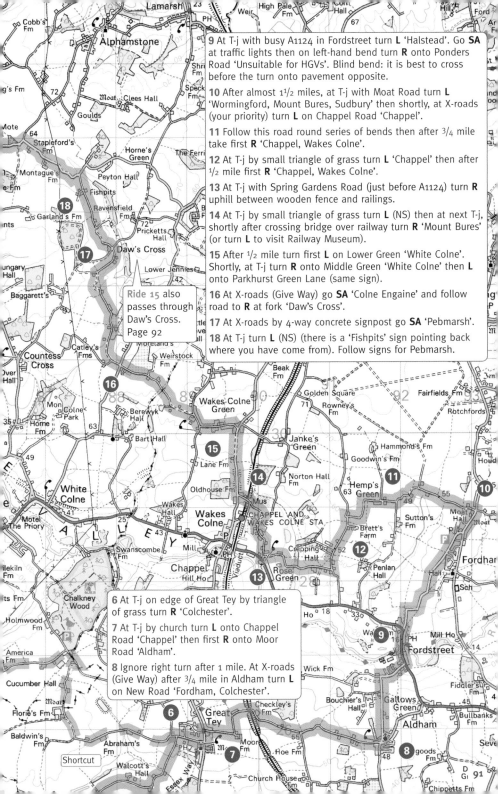

9 At T-j with busy A1124 in Fordstreet turn **L** 'Halstead'. Go **SA** at traffic lights then on left-hand bend turn **R** onto Ponders Road 'Unsuitable for HGVs'. Blind bend: it is best to cross before the turn onto pavement opposite.

10 After almost 1½ miles, at T-j with Moat Road turn **L** 'Wormingford, Mount Bures, Sudbury' then shortly, at X-roads (your priority) turn **L** on Chappel Road 'Chappel'.

11 Follow this road round series of bends then after ¾ mile take first **R** 'Chappel, Wakes Colne'.

12 At T-j by small triangle of grass turn **L** 'Chappel' then after ½ mile first **R** 'Chappel, Wakes Colne'.

13 At T-j with Spring Gardens Road (just before A1124) turn **R** uphill between wooden fence and railings.

14 At T-j by small triangle of grass turn **L** (NS) then at next T-j, shortly after crossing bridge over railway turn **R** 'Mount Bures' (or turn **L** to visit Railway Museum).

15 After ½ mile turn first **L** on Lower Green 'White Colne'. Shortly, at T-j turn **R** onto Middle Green 'White Colne' then **L** onto Parkhurst Green Lane (same sign).

16 At X-roads (Give Way) go **SA** 'Colne Engaine' and follow road to **R** at fork 'Daw's Cross'.

17 At X-roads by 4-way concrete signpost go **SA** 'Pebmarsh'.

18 At T-j turn **L** (NS) (there is a 'Fishpits' sign pointing back where you have come from). Follow signs for Pebmarsh.

Ride 15 also passes through Daw's Cross. Page 92

6 At T-j on edge of Great Tey by triangle of grass turn **R** 'Colchester'.

7 At T-j by church turn **L** onto Chappel Road 'Chappel' then first **R** onto Moor Road 'Aldham'.

8 Ignore right turn after 1 mile. At X-roads (Give Way) after ¾ mile in Aldham turn **L** on New Road 'Fordham, Colchester'.

Southwest from Sudbury to Castle Hedingham

S udbury is the birthplace of the painter Thomas Gainsborough, born in 1727. Gainsborough's House is half-timbered and dates from 1480, with an added Georgian front - it is now a museum with portraits and landscapes illustrating the artist's career. The ride starts by following the valley of the River Stour south through Henny Street and Lamarsh to Bures. Some of the farms on the tiny lanes southwest from here through Daw's Cross to Colne Engaine you

feel well might have inspired Gainsborough. The ride crosses from the Stour Valley to the Colne Valley at Colne Engaine before turning north through the Maplesteads and Castle Hedingham. The village is dominated by the towering Norman keep of Hedingham Castle, built around 1140 by the De Vere family who lived here for 500 years. There is a well-preserved banqueting hall and minstrels' gallery. The route heads west as far as Toppesfield before returning towards Sudbury via Bulmer

and a tiny narrow road called Sandy Lane for reasons that will become obvious.

Overview
On-road ● 33 miles / 53 kilometres ● Easy / Moderate

Start
The Leisure Centre, Sudbury (near the railway station). Sudbury is 15 miles northwest of Colchester

Parking
As above

Busy roads
● Care should be taken at the start / finish through Sudbury **1** to **2** and **21** to **22**

● A short section of the A1107 is used through Great Yeldham **18**

Terrain
Undulating

Nearest railway
Sudbury

Refreshments
Sudbury
Lots of choice

Lamarsh
Lamarsh Lion PH
T: 01787 227918

Bures
Lots of choice

Castle Hedingham
Lots of choice

Delvin End
Bottle Hall PH
T: 01787 462405

Great Yeldham
Waggon and Horses PH
T: 01787 237936
White Hart PH
T: 01787 237250

Map pages

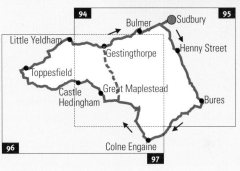

Other rides nearby

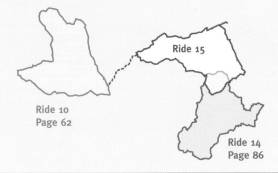

Ride 15

Ride 10
Page 62

Ride 14
Page 86

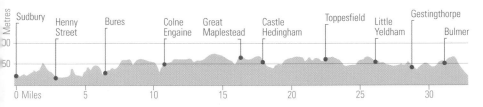

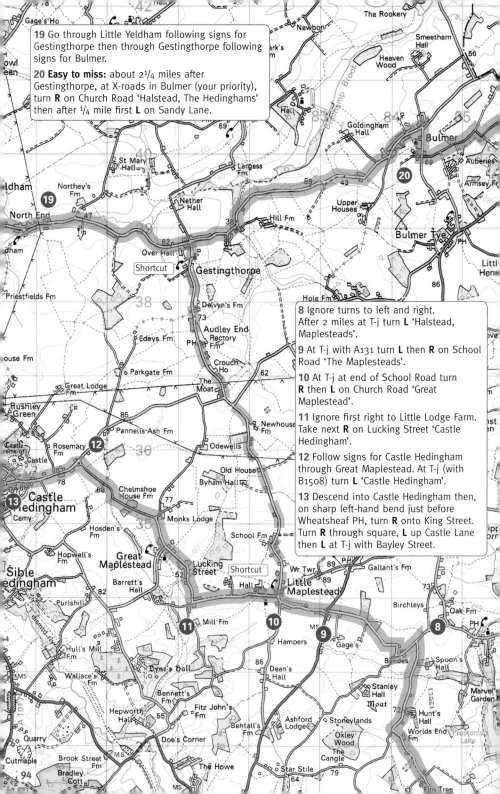

19 Go through Little Yeldham following signs for Gestingthorpe then through Gestingthorpe following signs for Bulmer.

20 Easy to miss: about 2¼ miles after Gestingthorpe, at X-roads in Bulmer (your priority), turn **R** on Church Road 'Halstead, The Hedinghams' then after ¼ mile first **L** on Sandy Lane.

8 Ignore turns to left and right. After 2 miles at T-j turn **L** 'Halstead, Maplesteads'.

9 At T-j with A131 turn **L** then **R** on School Road 'The Maplesteads'.

10 At T-j at end of School Road turn **R** then **L** on Church Road 'Great Maplestead'.

11 Ignore first right to Little Lodge Farm. Take next **R** on Lucking Street 'Castle Hedingham'.

12 Follow signs for Castle Hedingham through Great Maplestead. At T-j (with B1508) turn **L** 'Castle Hedingham'.

13 Descend into Castle Hedingham then, on sharp left-hand bend just before Wheatsheaf PH, turn **R** onto King Street. Turn **R** through square, **L** up Castle Lane then **L** at T-j with Bayley Street.

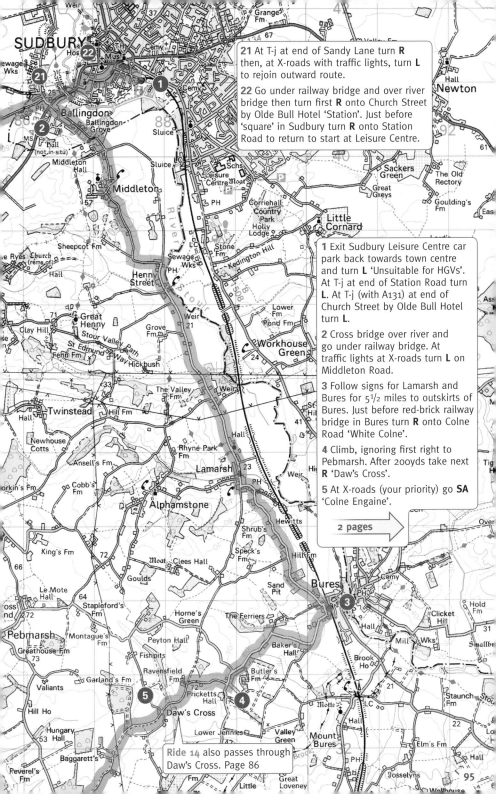

21 At T-j at end of Sandy Lane turn **R** then, at X-roads with traffic lights, turn **L** to rejoin outward route.

22 Go under railway bridge and over river bridge then turn first **R** onto Church Street by Olde Bull Hotel 'Station'. Just before 'square' in Sudbury turn **R** onto Station Road to return to start at Leisure Centre.

1 Exit Sudbury Leisure Centre car park back towards town centre and turn **L** 'Unsuitable for HGVs'. At T-j at end of Station Road turn **L**. At T-j (with A131) at end of Church Street by Olde Bull Hotel turn **L**.

2 Cross bridge over river and go under railway bridge. At traffic lights at X-roads turn **L** on Middleton Road.

3 Follow signs for Lamarsh and Bures for 5½ miles to outskirts of Bures. Just before red-brick railway bridge in Bures turn **R** onto Colne Road 'White Colne'.

4 Climb, ignoring first right to Pebmarsh. After 200yds take next **R** 'Daw's Cross'.

5 At X-roads (your priority) go **SA** 'Colne Engaine'.

2 pages ➡

Ride 14 also passes through Daw's Cross. Page 86

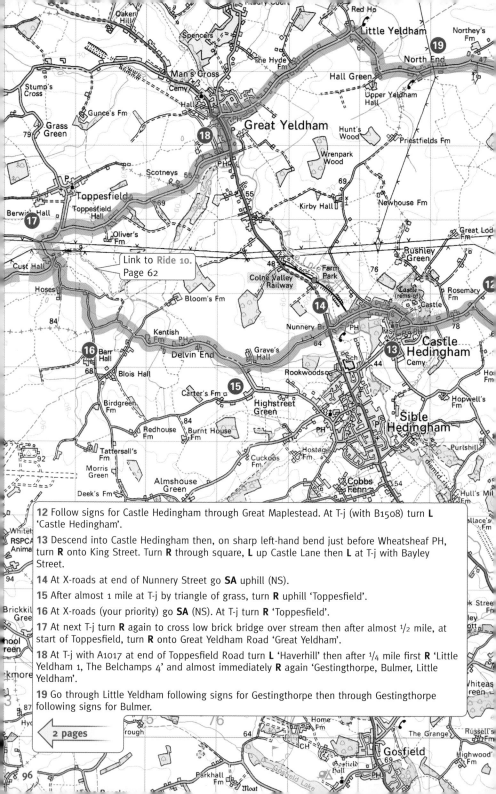

12 Follow signs for Castle Hedingham through Great Maplestead. At T-j (with B1508) turn **L** 'Castle Hedingham'.

13 Descend into Castle Hedingham then, on sharp left-hand bend just before Wheatsheaf PH, turn **R** onto King Street. Turn **R** through square, **L** up Castle Lane then **L** at T-j with Bayley Street.

14 At X-roads at end of Nunnery Street go **SA** uphill (NS).

15 After almost 1 mile at T-j by triangle of grass, turn **R** uphill 'Toppesfield'.

16 At X-roads (your priority) go **SA** (NS). At T-j turn **R** 'Toppesfield'.

17 At next T-j turn **R** again to cross low brick bridge over stream then after almost ½ mile, at start of Toppesfield, turn **R** onto Great Yeldham Road 'Great Yeldham'.

18 At T-j with A1017 at end of Toppesfield Road turn **L** 'Haverhill' then after ¼ mile first **R** 'Little Yeldham 1, The Belchamps 4' and almost immediately **R** again 'Gestingthorpe, Bulmer, Little Yeldham'.

19 Go through Little Yeldham following signs for Gestingthorpe then through Gestingthorpe following signs for Bulmer.

Link to **Ride 10.**
Page 62

2 pages

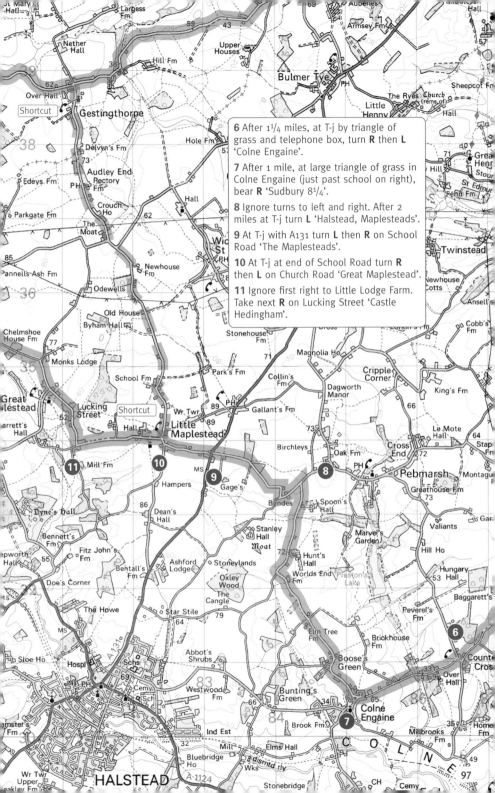

6 After 1¼ miles, at T-j by triangle of grass and telephone box, turn **R** then **L** 'Colne Engaine'.

7 After 1 mile, at large triangle of grass in Colne Engaine (just past school on right), bear **R** 'Sudbury 8¼'.

8 Ignore turns to left and right. After 2 miles at T-j turn **L** 'Halstead, Maplesteads'.

9 At T-j with A131 turn **L** then **R** on School Road 'The Maplesteads'.

10 At T-j at end of School Road turn **R** then **L** on Church Road 'Great Maplestead'.

11 Ignore first right to Little Lodge Farm. Take next **R** on Lucking Street 'Castle Hedingham'.

Aldbury, the Icknield Way & Berkhamsted Common

The ride starts from Aldbury, an attractive village set at the eastern end of the Chilterns. Steep tracks through woodland climb to the Bridgewater Monument in the Ashridge Estate, erected in 1831 in memory of the canal pioneer, the 3rd Duke of Bridgewater. A fine contouring track high up the escarpment leads towards Ivinghoe Beacon, one of several beacon points established during the reign of Elizabeth I to summon men in case of Spanish invasion. Drop down on-road to the track that leads towards the church at Edlesborough, set dramatically against the skyline. A very steep climb to Whipsnade follows which will involve some pushing. Follow around the edge of the zoo with the odd glimpse of exotic

animals. A short rough field edge section ends in Hudnall where things improve with a combination of disused county roads (including an extraordinary section beyond the church in Nettleden between high flint walls and beneath a bridge). The ride soon reaches Berkhamsted Common and follows lovely woodland trails for almost 5 miles back to Aldbury.

NB Hertfordshire mud is renowned for its sticky, cement-like quality. Although every attempt has been made to use tracks that are passable for large parts of the year, you are likely to encounter mud at various points and this will be much worse from late autumn to late spring and after any particularly wet periods.

Overview

Off-road ● 20 miles / 32 kilometres ● Strenuous

Start
The Greyhound Inn, Aldbury,
3 miles east of Tring, 10 miles
east of Aylesbury

Parking
Car park at the north end of
the village - follow signs

Busy roads
● The B489 beneath Ivinghoe
Beacon **6**

● The B4506 / B4540 east of
Whipsnade **9** to **11**

Nearest railway
Tring

Refreshments
Aldbury
Greyhound Inn
T: 01442 851228
Valiant Trooper PH
T: 01442 851203

Edlesborough
Bell PH
T: 01525 220314

Whipsnade
Old Hunters Lodge PH
T: 01582 872228

Frithsden
Alford Arms PH
T: 01442 864480

Map pages

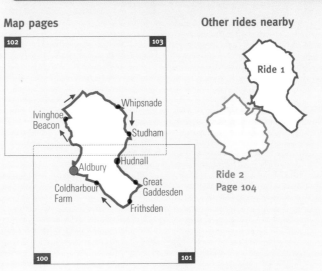

Other rides nearby

Ride 1

Ride 2
Page 104

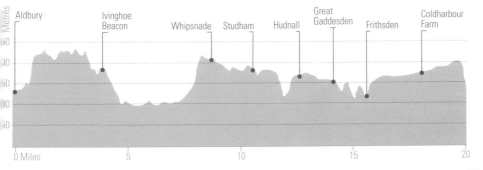

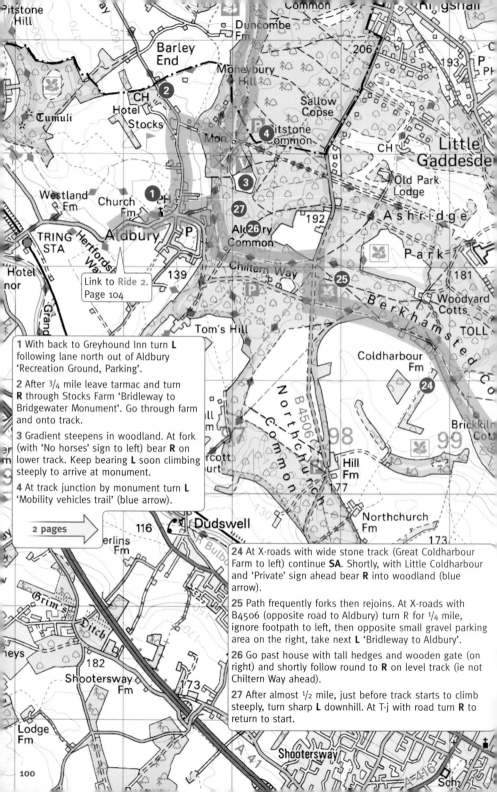

1 With back to Greyhound Inn turn **L** following lane north out of Aldbury 'Recreation Ground, Parking'.

2 After 3/4 mile leave tarmac and turn **R** through Stocks Farm 'Bridleway to Bridgewater Monument'. Go through farm and onto track.

3 Gradient steepens in woodland. At fork (with 'No horses' sign to left) bear **R** on lower track. Keep bearing **L** soon climbing steeply to arrive at monument.

4 At track junction by monument turn **L** 'Mobility vehicles trail' (blue arrow).

2 pages →

24 At X-roads with wide stone track (Great Coldharbour Farm to left) continue **SA**. Shortly, with Little Coldharbour and 'Private' sign ahead bear **R** into woodland (blue arrow).

25 Path frequently forks then rejoins. At X-roads with B4506 (opposite road to Aldbury) turn R for 1/4 mile, ignore footpath to left, then opposite small gravel parking area on the right, take next **L** 'Bridleway to Aldbury'.

26 Go past house with tall hedges and wooden gate (on right) and shortly follow round to **R** on level track (ie not Chiltern Way ahead).

27 After almost 1/2 mile, just before track starts to climb steeply, turn sharp **L** downhill. At T-j with road turn **R** to return to start.

Link to **Ride 2**. Page 104

18 At T-j with road bear **L**. At X-roads by 'Little Gaddesden' sign go **SA** (no through road).

19 Tarmac turns to track then back to tarmac. At T-j turn sharply **R** steeply uphill.

20 Climb then fast descent. At T-j in Nettleden with church ahead turn **R** then **L** 'Unsuitable for motors'. Amazing high brick and flint walls either side of steep track.

21 At T-j by Alford Arms PH turn **L**. At T-j after 150yds turn **R** 'Potten End, Berkhamsted'.

22 Steady climb. After ¹/₂ mile, and shortly after passing Vicarage Road on left, turn **R** through small gravel layby by 3-way sign 'Bridleway' and turn **R** at fork.

23 Follow track along edge of wood crossing golf course as waymarked. At road go **SA** and continue in same direction through woodland following blue arrows on yellow-topped posts.

5 Easy woodland track. After 2¼ miles, at T-j with road turn **L**.

6 Fast descent. At T-j with B489 turn **R** 'Dunstable'. Brief climb then after almost ½ mile first **L** 'Ivinghoe Aston'.

7 Easy to miss: after ¾ mile, towards bottom of descent, at 'Ivinghoe Aston' village sign on white gate, turn **R** on track through yellow metal bollards 'Bridleway'.

8 At X-roads by church and Bell PH in Edlesborough go **SA** 'Village Centre' then second **R** on to Pebblemoor.

9 After ⅓ mile, at end of houses, on sharp right-hand bend, turn **L** onto lane (NS). Go through ford, climb then after 200yds take first road **R** (NS). Shortly at T-j turn **R** (NS).

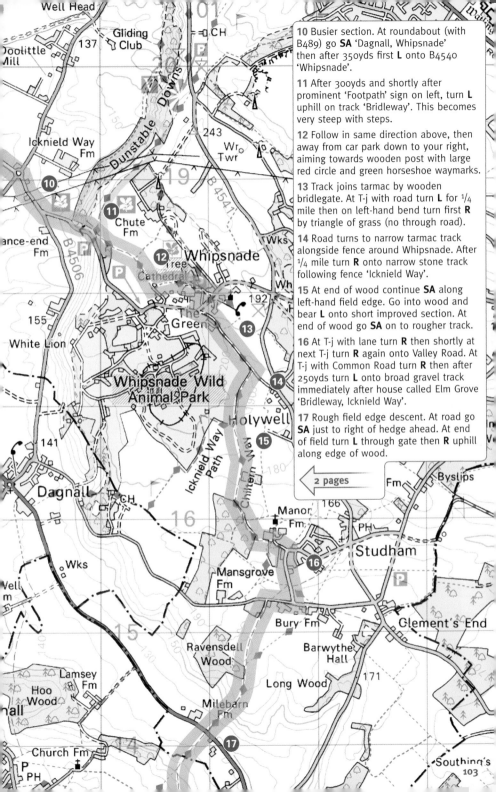

10 Busier section. At roundabout (with B489) go **SA** 'Dagnall, Whipsnade' then after 350yds first **L** onto B4540 'Whipsnade'.

11 After 300yds and shortly after prominent 'Footpath' sign on left, turn **L** uphill on track 'Bridleway'. This becomes very steep with steps.

12 Follow in same direction above, then away from car park down to your right, aiming towards wooden post with large red circle and green horseshoe waymarks.

13 Track joins tarmac by wooden bridlegate. At T-j with road turn **L** for 1/4 mile then on left-hand bend turn first **R** by triangle of grass (no through road).

14 Road turns to narrow tarmac track alongside fence around Whipsnade. After 1/4 mile turn **R** onto narrow stone track following fence 'Icknield Way'.

15 At end of wood continue **SA** along left-hand field edge. Go into wood and bear **L** onto short improved section. At end of wood go **SA** on to rougher track.

16 At T-j with lane turn **R** then shortly at next T-j turn **R** again onto Valley Road. At T-j with Common Road turn **R** then after 250yds turn **L** onto broad gravel track immediately after house called Elm Grove 'Bridleway, Icknield Way'.

17 Rough field edge descent. At road go **SA** just to right of hedge ahead. At end of field turn **L** through gate then **R** uphill along edge of wood.

2 pages

Woodland & hills above Tring & Berkhamsted

Although Tring and Berkhamsted may seem two somewhat improbable centres for off-road cycling in Hertfordshire, there are many fine bridleways through the woods above the two towns and, if all else fails, the Grand Union Canal with its generally well-maintained towpath runs between them. The ride leaves Tring to the east, crosses the canal and soon joins an excellent stretch of improved bridleway. Climb up on to Aldbury Common and around the edge of Northchurch Common. There is an abrupt change of scenery as you pass from wooded bridleway straight into the centre of Berkhamsted. Climb out of the town, under the A41 bypass and head off-road to the scenic ruins of Marlin Chapel. A lovely disused county road through woodland drops you on the road that runs through Cholesbury. From here you climb to the highest point of the ride at Hastoe and the best descent of the day back to Tring. Other off-road options in the area include the waymarked trails in Wendover Woods (easy) and Aston Hill (hard). Go to www.forestry.gov.uk/wendoverwoods or www.rideastonhill.co.uk

NB Hertfordshire mud is renowned for its sticky, cement-like quality. Although every attempt has been made to use tracks that are passable for a large part of the year, you are likely to encounter mud at various points and this will be much worse from late autumn to late spring and after any particularly wet periods.

Overview
Off-road ● 17 miles / 27 kilometres ● Moderate / Strenuous

Start
The car park in the centre of Tring, on the High Street. (Alternatively, the Sports Centre in Berkhamsted)

Parking
As above

Busy roads
The section through Berkhamsted is mainly on residential roads **12** to **14**

Nearest railway
Tring or Berkhamsted

Refreshments
Tring
Lots of choice

Berkhamsted
Lots of choice

Aldbury (just off the route)
Greyhound Inn
T: 01442 851228
Valiant Trooper PH
T: 01442 851203

Cholesbury
Full Moon PH
T: 01494 758959

Map pages

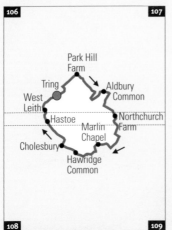

Other rides nearby

Ride 1
Page 98

Ride 2

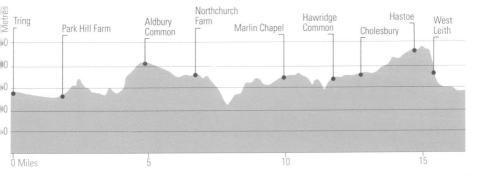

105

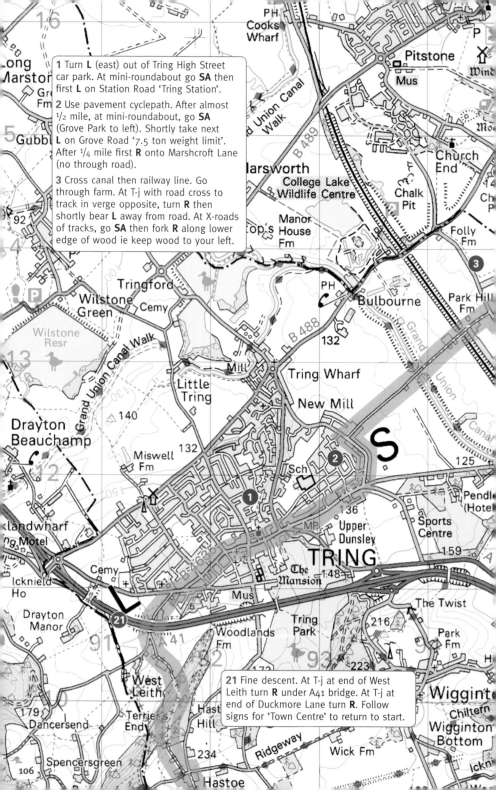

1 Turn **L** (east) out of Tring High Street car park. At mini-roundabout go **SA** then first **L** on Station Road 'Tring Station'.

2 Use pavement cyclepath. After almost ½ mile, at mini-roundabout, go **SA** (Grove Park to left). Shortly take next **L** on Grove Road '7.5 ton weight limit'. After ¼ mile first **R** onto Marshcroft Lane (no through road).

3 Cross canal then railway line. Go through farm. At T-j with road cross to track in verge opposite, turn **R** then shortly bear **L** away from road. At X-roads of tracks, go **SA** then fork **R** along lower edge of wood ie keep wood to your left.

21 Fine descent. At T-j at end of West Leith turn **R** under A41 bridge. At T-j at end of Duckmore Lane turn **R**. Follow signs for 'Town Centre' to return to start.

4 Carry on in same direction as track enters woodland. After ¹/₂ mile, at X-roads of tracks go **SA** 'Bridleway'. At road bear **L** (in effect **SA**).

5 After 400yds, on sharp left-hand bend, bear **R** onto broad gravel track 'Bridleway to Aldbury Common' following close to hedge to your left.

6 At T-j with road turn **R** then after almost ¹/₂ mile take first major track to **L** 'Byway' through gate and alongside row of trees. Go past barn, climb along field edge then follow grassy track as it swings **L** across field towards gate into wood 'Bridleway'.

7 Climb through wood, join wider stone track by barn and bear **L** to continue uphill through farm onto tarmac. At T-j with road on steep bend turn **R** uphill.

8 Easy to miss: ignore first bridleway on right after ¹/₄ mile. After further ¹/₂ mile, just past timber buildings of 'Base Camp' on your left, and 100yds before road junction (Give Way), turn **R** at metal post 'Bridleway to Norcott Hill ³/₄'.

9 Continue in same direction on broad grass and earth track. Exit woodland by square wooden post with blue arrows and 'Ashridge Estate' waymarks. Keep wood to your right. The wide track swings **L** across grassy expanse between clumps of trees.

10 At T-j with road turn **R** then shortly after passing Hill Farm and chevrons on right-hand bend, bear **L** into woodland 'Byway no. 39'. At X-roads (Northchurch Farm to left) go **SA** onto wide track opposite (red arrow).

2 pages

Link to Ride 1.
Page 98

17 Steep climb. Go past Hill Farm. Ignore bridleway through gate to right. Fine descent. At T-j with road by black wooden house turn **R** 'Cholesbury'. At T-j with more major road at end of Stoney Lane turn **R**.

18 Go past Full Moon PH in Cholesbury then shortly after cricket pitch and pavilion, turn **R** 'Wigginton, Tring'. Ignore first left on Shire Lane. Take next **L** on Kiln Road 'Hastoe, Tring'.

19 After 250yds, on right-hand bend, bear **L** (in effect **SA**) through gate onto broad track 'Byway to Hastoe'.

20 At junction with major road turn **L** then **R** by triangle of grass 'Byway'. Shortly at fork pass to **R** of house (red arrow) 'No motorbikes'.

2 pages

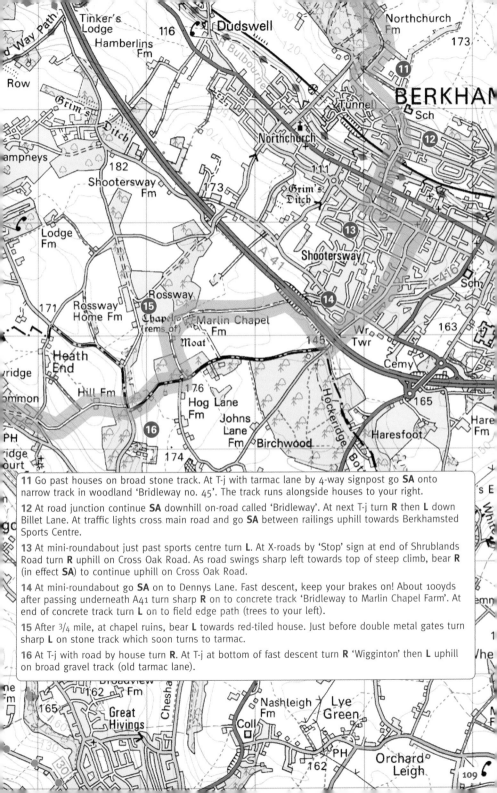

11 Go past houses on broad stone track. At T-j with tarmac lane by 4-way signpost go **SA** onto narrow track in woodland 'Bridleway no. 45'. The track runs alongside houses to your right.

12 At road junction continue **SA** downhill on-road called 'Bridleway'. At next T-j turn **R** then **L** down Billet Lane. At traffic lights cross main road and go **SA** between railings uphill towards Berkhamsted Sports Centre.

13 At mini-roundabout just past sports centre turn **L**. At X-roads by 'Stop' sign at end of Shrublands Road turn **R** uphill on Cross Oak Road. As road swings sharp left towards top of steep climb, bear **R** (in effect **SA**) to continue uphill on Cross Oak Road.

14 At mini-roundabout go **SA** on to Dennys Lane. Fast descent, keep your brakes on! About 100yds after passing underneath A41 turn sharp **R** on to concrete track 'Bridleway to Marlin Chapel Farm'. At end of concrete track turn **L** on to field edge path (trees to your left).

15 After 3/4 mile, at chapel ruins, bear **L** towards red-tiled house. Just before double metal gates turn sharp **L** on stone track which soon turns to tarmac.

16 At T-j with road by house turn **R**. At T-j at bottom of fast descent turn **R** 'Wigginton' then **L** uphill on broad gravel track (old tarmac lane).

Woodland tracks & the Grand Union Canal from Hemel Hempstead

For an area so close to Hemel Hempstead, Chesham and Amersham, this ride has a surprisingly rural, wooded feel to it. The ride starts with a long section along the towpath of the Grand Union Canal through Kings Langley. Pass underneath the M25 on the towpath, then over it as you climb from Hunton Bridge up towards Commonwood. The avenue of trees soon after

crossing the motorway seems to welcome you to a different world from the traffic mayhem you have just passed over. Permissive bridleways, tiny lanes and unclassified roads take you close to Flaunden above the valley of the River Chess to the east of Chesham. Briefly touch tarmac through Botley before diving off onto more woodland tracks. Wiggle your way through Bovingdon for the final off-road descent

right back down into the heart of Hemel Hempstead. This is a complicated ride full of instructions and will get better and better as you do it a second and third time and know what to do at the myriad junctions. There is such a dense network of lane and tracks in the area that you may wish to customise it to suit your own needs.

Overview
Off-road ● 21 miles / 34 kilometres ● Moderate

Start
Durrants Hill car park, right next to the Grand Union Canal in Hemel Hempstead, just east of the junction of the A4251 London Road with the A414 Two Waters Road. The car park lies at the junction of Frogmore Road with Durrants Hill Road - use the internet for more detail. Alternatively park near Apsley Marina

Parking
As above

Busy roads
● Short busy section after leaving canal towpath near Hunton Bridge ❷ to ❸

● The London Road in Hemel Hempstead right at the end of the ride ㉒

Nearest railway
Kings Langley (on the route), Little Chalfont (just south of the route near Latimer)

Refreshments
Hemel Hempstead & canal towpath
Lots of choice

Commonwood
Cart & Horses PH
T: 01923 263763

Belsize
Plough PH
T: 01923 262261

Ley Hill
The Swan PH
T: 01494 783075
Crown PH
T: 01494 783910

Bovingdon
Lots of choice

Map pages

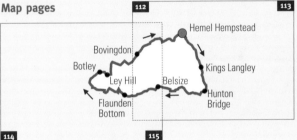

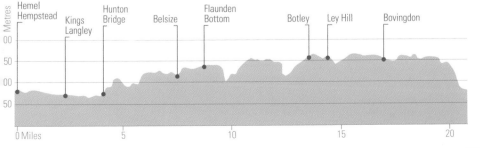

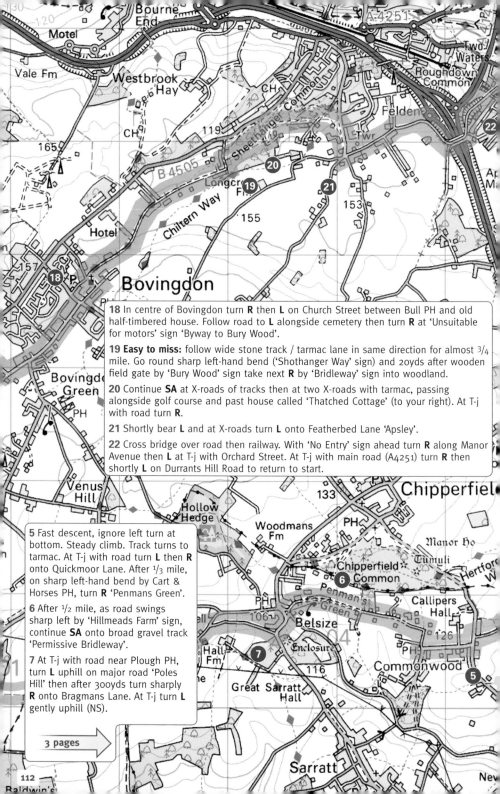

18 In centre of Bovingdon turn **R** then **L** on Church Street between Bull PH and old half-timbered house. Follow road to **L** alongside cemetery then turn **R** at 'Unsuitable for motors' sign 'Byway to Bury Wood'.

19 Easy to miss: follow wide stone track / tarmac lane in same direction for almost ³⁄₄ mile. Go round sharp left-hand bend ('Shothanger Way' sign) and 20yds after wooden field gate by 'Bury Wood' sign take next **R** by 'Bridleway' sign into woodland.

20 Continue **SA** at X-roads of tracks then at two X-roads with tarmac, passing alongside golf course and past house called 'Thatched Cottage' (to your right). At T-j with road turn **R**.

21 Shortly bear **L** and at X-roads turn **L** onto Featherbed Lane 'Apsley'.

22 Cross bridge over road then railway. With 'No Entry' sign ahead turn **R** along Manor Avenue then **L** at T-j with Orchard Street. At T-j with main road (A4251) turn **R** then shortly **L** on Durrants Hill Road to return to start.

5 Fast descent, ignore left turn at bottom. Steady climb. Track turns to tarmac. At T-j with road turn **L** then **R** onto Quickmoor Lane. After ¹⁄₃ mile, on sharp left-hand bend by Cart & Horses PH, turn **R** 'Penmans Green'.

6 After ¹⁄₂ mile, as road swings sharp left by 'Hillmeads Farm' sign, continue **SA** onto broad gravel track 'Permissive Bridleway'.

7 At T-j with road near Plough PH, turn **L** uphill on major road 'Poles Hill' then after 300yds turn sharply **R** onto Bragmans Lane. At T-j turn **L** gently uphill (NS).

3 pages

1 Join Grand Union Canal towpath and head southeast towards Kings Langley (water to your left).

2 Follow for 4½ miles, crossing sides as necessary and passing beneath massive M25 bridge. At round-arched black-brick bridge no. 162, with sign for Dog & Partridge PH, leave towpath and turn **R** onto road. At X-roads (traffic lights) with A41 go **SA** uphill past church.

3 Climb on busy road. After ½ mile, shortly after passing Langleybury Farm, turn **R** onto lane and bridge over M25 'Bridleway to Bucks Hill'.

4 After ½ mile, on sharp right-hand bend, with black and white timber house ahead, bear **L** onto broad gravel track.

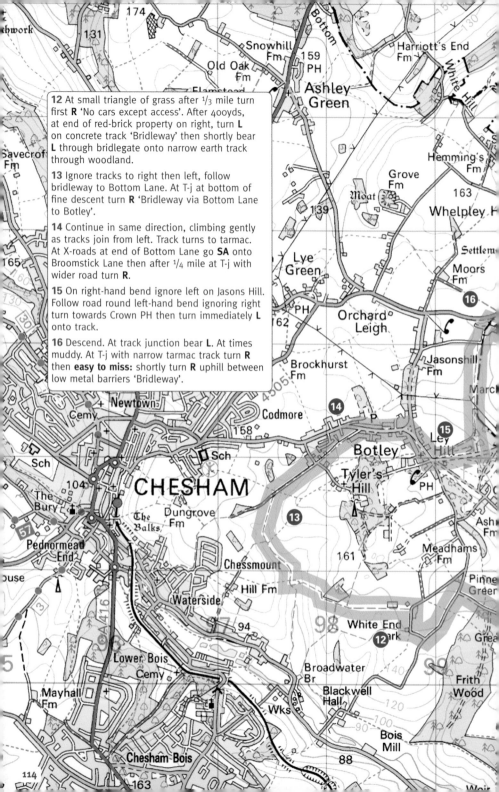

12 At small triangle of grass after ⅓ mile turn first **R** 'No cars except access'. After 400yds, at end of red-brick property on right, turn **L** on concrete track 'Bridleway' then shortly bear **L** through bridlegate onto narrow earth track through woodland.

13 Ignore tracks to right then left, follow bridleway to Bottom Lane. At T-j at bottom of fine descent turn **R** 'Bridleway via Bottom Lane to Botley'.

14 Continue in same direction, climbing gently as tracks join from left. Track turns to tarmac. At X-roads at end of Bottom Lane go **SA** onto Broomstick Lane then after ¼ mile at T-j with wider road turn **R**.

15 On right-hand bend ignore left on Jasons Hill. Follow road round left-hand bend ignoring right turn towards Crown PH then turn immediately **L** onto track.

16 Descend. At track junction bear **L**. At times muddy. At T-j with narrow tarmac track turn **R** then **easy to miss:** shortly turn **R** uphill between low metal barriers 'Bridleway'.

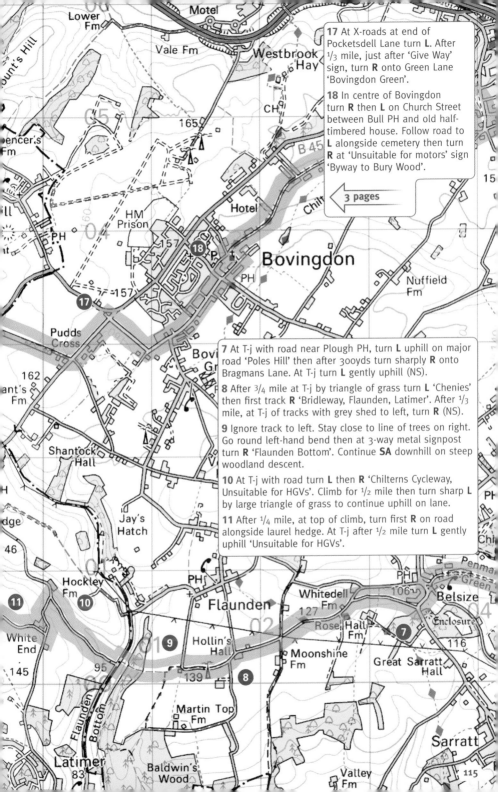

17 At X-roads at end of Pocketsdell Lane turn **L**. After 1/3 mile, just after 'Give Way' sign, turn **R** onto Green Lane 'Bovingdon Green'.

18 In centre of Bovingdon turn **R** then **L** on Church Street between Bull PH and old half-timbered house. Follow road to **L** alongside cemetery then turn **R** at 'Unsuitable for motors' sign 'Byway to Bury Wood'.

3 pages

7 At T-j with road near Plough PH, turn **L** uphill on major road 'Poles Hill' then after 300yds turn sharply **R** onto Bragmans Lane. At T-j turn **L** gently uphill (NS).

8 After 3/4 mile at T-j by triangle of grass turn **L** 'Chenies' then first track **R** 'Bridleway, Flaunden, Latimer'. After 1/3 mile, at T-j of tracks with grey shed to left, turn **R** (NS).

9 Ignore track to left. Stay close to line of trees on right. Go round left-hand bend then at 3-way metal signpost turn **R** 'Flaunden Bottom'. Continue **SA** downhill on steep woodland descent.

10 At T-j with road turn **L** then **R** 'Chilterns Cycleway, Unsuitable for HGVs'. Climb for 1/2 mile then turn sharp **L** by large triangle of grass to continue uphill on lane.

11 After 1/4 mile, at top of climb, turn first **R** on road alongside laurel hedge. At T-j after 1/2 mile turn **L** gently uphill 'Unsuitable for HGVs'.

Great Offley & the Icknield Way

Although it may seem a slightly unlikely centre, the village of Great Offley, set squarely between Luton and Hitchin, not only boasts three pubs but has within a five-mile radius of the village dozens of miles of good quality tracks ideal for off-road cycling, whether these be bridleways, byways or old, unclassified county roads that have fallen into a state of benign neglect.

Most famous of these is the Icknield Way which runs from the end of the Ridgeway at Goring on Thames and connects with the Peddars Way at Thetford, making it part of a track that used to run all the way from Dorset to the Wash. The highest point of the ride is reached on the Icknield Way at the top of Telegraph Hill, followed by a fine, gentle descent to the road. Hitchin is skirted on three sides before the lanes link up with an old county road that climbs over 300 feet back to Great Offley. A quick glance at the map shows that there are plenty more options for shorter circuits by using the network of bridleways around Little Offley (north of the A505) or southeast from Great Offley towards Preston.

Overview
Off-road ● 20 miles / 32 kilometres ● Moderate

Start
Green Man PH, Great Offley, just off the A505 between Luton and Hitchin

Parking
On-street parking - please show consideration

Busy roads
The road from the end of the Icknield Way section near to Letchworth south to the roundabout with the A505 to the east of Hitchin can be busy **12** to **13**

Nearest railway
Hitchin

Refreshments
Great Offley
Green Man PH
T: 01462 768256
Gloucester Arms PH
T: 01462 769769
Red Lion PH
T: 01462 768281

Lilley
Lilley Arms PH
T: 01462 768371

Pirton
Motte and Bailey PH
T: 01462 712641
Fox PH
T: 01462 713770

Gosmore
Bird in Hand PH
T: 01462 432079
Bull PH
T: 01462 440035

Map pages

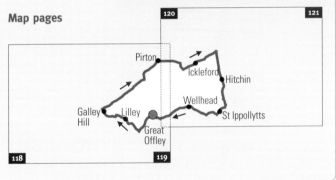

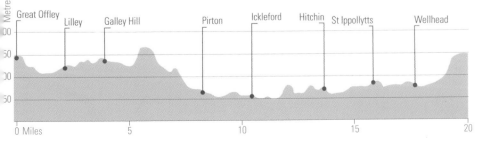

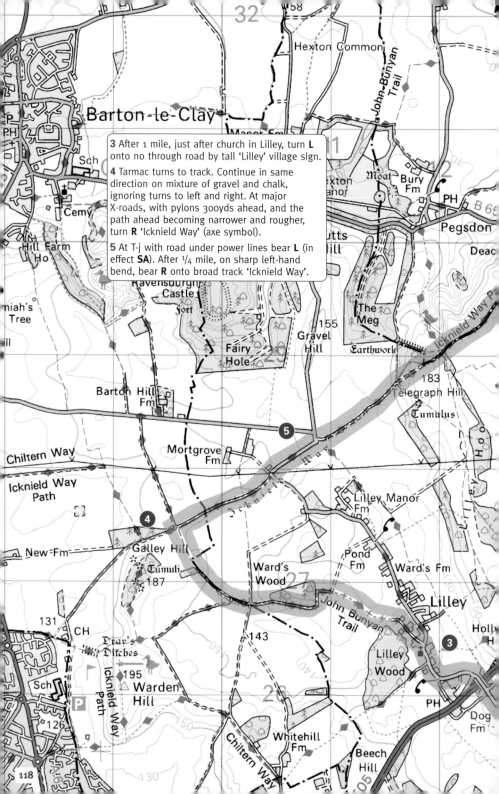

3 After 1 mile, just after church in Lilley, turn **L** onto no through road by tall 'Lilley' village sign.

4 Tarmac turns to track. Continue in same direction on mixture of gravel and chalk, ignoring turns to left and right. At major X-roads, with pylons 300yds ahead, and the path ahead becoming narrower and rougher, turn **R** 'Icknield Way' (axe symbol).

5 At T-j with road under power lines bear **L** (in effect **SA**). After 1/4 mile, on sharp left-hand bend, bear **R** onto broad track 'Icknield Way'.

6 Long climb, at times steep, ignoring turnings to the right. Long gentle descent. At T-j with busy road (B655) turn **R** for 300yds then turn **L*** onto narrow track following line of telegraph poles 'Bridleway, Icknield Way'.

*OR *for shortcut, turn **R** here onto broad track. At T-j of tracks turn **R** to return to Great Offley.*

7 At T-j of tracks at end of field turn **R** downhill 'Bridleway, Icknield Way'.

8 At X-roads with road go **SA** onto Great Green. At X-roads with Fox PH ahead turn **R**. At next X-roads go **SA** onto Hambridge Way.

1 page ➡

1 With back to Green Man PH in Great Offley turn **R** then at X-roads at end of High Street turn **L** 'Lilley'. After 1/4 mile, on right-hand bend shortly after bus shelter, turn **L** (NS).

2 Long gentle descent. At T-j turn **R** 'Lilley, Hexton'.

21 Tarmac shortly turns to chalk and earth track. Gradient steepens after 1 mile. At T-j with road near Red Lion PH in Great Offley turn **R** to return to start.

Shortcut

Shortcut

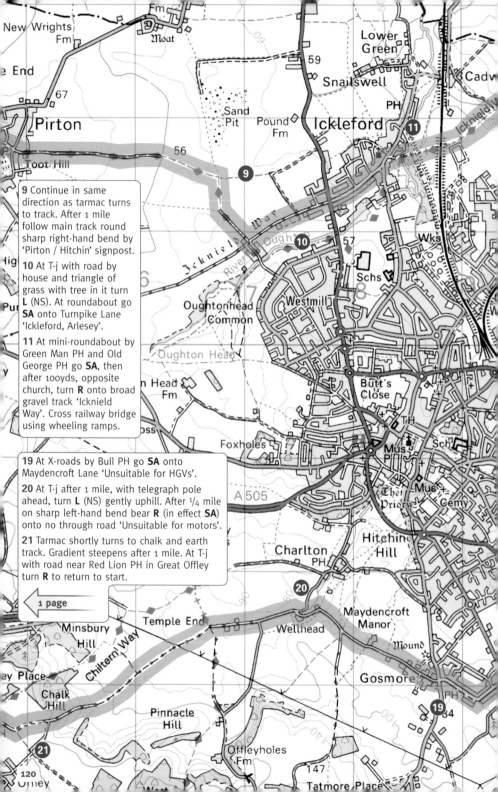

9 Continue in same direction as tarmac turns to track. After 1 mile follow main track round sharp right-hand bend by 'Pirton / Hitchin' signpost.

10 At T-j with road by house and triangle of grass with tree in it turn **L** (NS). At roundabout go **SA** onto Turnpike Lane 'Ickleford, Arlesey'.

11 At mini-roundabout by Green Man PH and Old George PH go **SA**, then after 100yds, opposite church, turn **R** onto broad gravel track 'Icknield Way'. Cross railway bridge using wheeling ramps.

19 At X-roads by Bull PH go **SA** onto Maydencroft Lane 'Unsuitable for HGVs'.

20 At T-j after 1 mile, with telegraph pole ahead, turn **L** (NS) gently uphill. After ¼ mile on sharp left-hand bend bear **R** (in effect **SA**) onto no through road 'Unsuitable for motors'.

21 Tarmac shortly turns to chalk and earth track. Gradient steepens after 1 mile. At T-j with road near Red Lion PH in Great Offley turn **R** to return to start.

← 1 page

12 Long steady climb. At T-j with road turn **R**.

13 Busier section. Climb, descend, climb. At roundabout with A505 use cycle island to go **SA** onto Queenswood Drive. After 350yds at X-roads go **SA** onto Kingswood Avenue.

14 After ¹/₂ mile at bottom of hill on sharp right-hand bend, bear **L** onto narrow track into woodland.

15 At X-roads with road go **SA** onto broad gravel track past Spring Cottage.

16 At T-j with road turn **R** gently downhill towards pylons (NS). At roundabout turn **R** then just before bus shelter turn **L** downhill onto track 'Bridleway to St Ippollytts'.

17 Go under road bridge and follow main track as it swings **L** over small bridge over stream.

18 Climb. At T-j with lane turn **R**. Follow road to **R** past church, then opposite school turn **L** downhill 'Gosmore, Preston'. At X-roads with B656 go **SA** 'Gosmore'.

Southwest from Hertford on woodland tracks & the Cole Green Way

Encircled by built-up areas running alongside the A1 and A10 and bounded to the north by the A414 and the south by the M25, there is nevertheless a patch of countryside lying to the southwest of Hertford that offers many miles of fine off-road riding along broad gravel tracks through woodland. This short ride links together lanes and byways from the southwestern corner of Hertford through Brickendon to Newgate Street. The middle section runs along predominantly quiet lanes, including one which appears to have an identity crisis - it is signed 'Berkhamsted' on one side of the road and 'Berkhampstead' on the other! Just before Cole Green you find yourself at the start of the Cole Greenway, a magnificent conversion of an old dismantled railway line for recreational use. This drops you right back at the start. Hertfordshire is blessed with many miles of easy traffic-free riding, whether on the Lee Navigation towpath (see Ride 6 page 38), the Grand Union Canal towpath or on railway paths further west such as the Albanway from St Albans to Hatfield, the Nickey Line from Harpenden to Hemel Hempstead or the Ayot Greenway from Wheathampstead.

Overview
Off-road ● 15 miles / 24 kilometres ● Easy

Start
Hertford Town Football Club, West Street, Hertford (just off the A414 Hatfield road past car showroom). Follow West Street for 400 yards. Shortly after the houses end on the left, on a left-hand bend, turn right down a tarmac lane

Parking
As above

Busy roads
The road south of Letty Green, just before the start of the railway path, is at times busy **12** to **13**

Nearest railway
Hertford

Refreshments
Hertford
Lots of choice

Brickendon
Farmer's Boy PH
T: 01992 511610

Newgate Street
Coach & Horses PH
T: 01707 872326
Crown PH
T: 01707 872107

Cole Green
Cowpers Arms PH
T: 01707 330202

Map pages

Hertford
Letty Green
Howe Green
Little Berkhamsted
Brickendon
Old Claypits Farm
Newgate Street

124   **125**

THE FARMERS BOY
FREE HOUSE

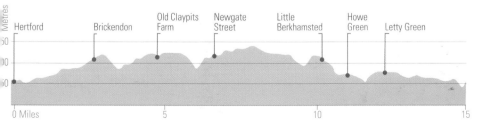

Metres

Hertford   Brickendon   Old Claypits Farm   Newgate Street   Little Berkhamsted   Howe Green   Letty Green

0 Miles   5   10   15

8 Tarmac turns to track. At T-j with road turn **L** then **R** onto Cucumber Lane.

9 Easy to miss: after almost 1¼ miles turn first **R** onto Berkhamsted Lane.

10 Descend then climb. Shortly after start of 30mph speed limit turn **L** onto track by white gate (drive to Terra Cottage) 'Bridleway'.

11 At bottom of hill cross stream then immediately turn **R** onto gravel track. Emerge at concrete road and bear **L** (haulage company to right).

12 Continue in same direction, go through bridlegate adjacent to wide metal gates, then at X-roads at end of Bedwell Avenue go **SA** '7.5 ton weight limit'.

13 After 1 mile, immediately after passing beneath railway bridge and before Cowpers Arms PH, turn **R** through car park and onto railway path.

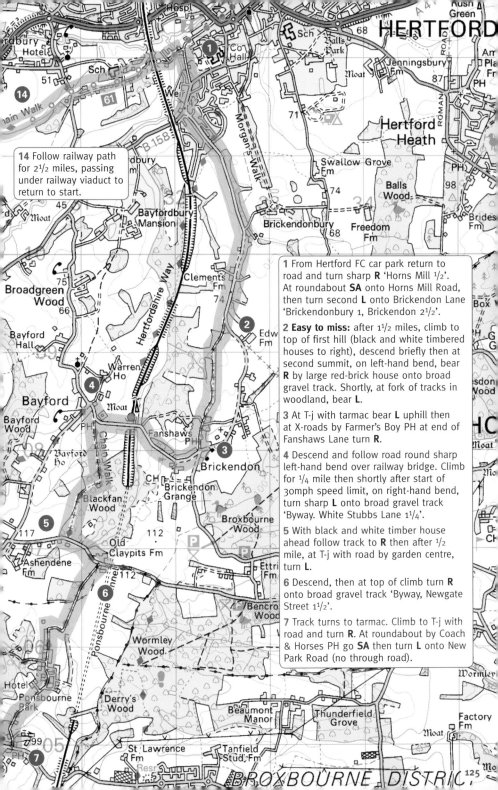

14 Follow railway path for 2½ miles, passing under railway viaduct to return to start.

1 From Hertford FC car park return to road and turn sharp **R** 'Horns Mill ½'. At roundabout **SA** onto Horns Mill Road, then turn second **L** onto Brickendon Lane 'Brickendonbury 1, Brickendon 2½'.

2 **Easy to miss:** after 1½ miles, climb to top of first hill (black and white timbered houses to right), descend briefly then at second summit, on left-hand bend, bear **R** by large red-brick house onto broad gravel track. Shortly, at fork of tracks in woodland, bear **L**.

3 At T-j with tarmac bear **L** uphill then at X-roads by Farmer's Boy PH at end of Fanshaws Lane turn **R**.

4 Descend and follow road round sharp left-hand bend over railway bridge. Climb for ¼ mile then shortly after start of 30mph speed limit, on right-hand bend, turn sharp **L** onto broad gravel track 'Byway. White Stubbs Lane 1¼'.

5 With black and white timber house ahead follow track to **R** then after ½ mile, at T-j with road by garden centre, turn **L**.

6 Descend, then at top of climb turn **R** onto broad gravel track 'Byway, Newgate Street 1½'.

7 Track turns to tarmac. Climb to T-j with road and turn **R**. At roundabout by Coach & Horses PH go **SA** then turn **L** onto New Park Road (no through road).

125

Notes